Catch Your Star

Top Experts Share Insights
for Lifelong Fulfillment

THRIVE Publishing®
A Division of PowerDynamics Publishing, Inc.
San Francisco, California
www.thrivebooks.com

ISBN: 978-0-9850828-9-5

Library of Congress Control Number: 2013943003
Printed in the United States of America on acid-free paper.

We Dedicate
This Book to You...

---

our reader; a woman who recognizes the power of learning from others on her journey to personal development, fulfillment and success. We salute you for investing in yourself and embracing the wisdom of others to enhance your life. We celebrate your commitment to being the best you can be!

The Co-Authors of *Catch Your Star*

Table of Contents

Acknowledgements

Expressing appreciation is a key part of catching your star. Before we share our wisdom and experience with you, we have a few people to thank for turning our vision for this book into a reality.

This book is the brilliant concept of Caterina Rando, the founder of THRIVE Publishing™ and a respected business strategist and coach, with whom many of us have worked to grow our businesses. Working closely with many life coaches, consultants and other professionals, she realized how valuable the knowledge they possessed would be to those people wanting to truly catch their star. The result was putting our ideas into a comprehensive book on women's personal development.

Without Caterina's "take action" spirit, her positive attitude and her commitment to excellence, you would not be reading this book of which we are all so proud. She was supported by a dedicated team who worked diligently to put together the best possible book for you. We are truly grateful for everyone's stellar contribution.

To Karen Gargiulo, who served as the project manager and copy editor for this book, we appreciate your patient guidance, thoughtful advice and genuine enthusiasm for our work, and we are truly grateful.

To Tammy Tribble and Noël Voskuil, our designers extraordinaire, who brought their creative talents to the cover and book layout, thank you both for your enthusiasm, problem solving and attention to detail throughout this project.

To Susan Rich and Rua Necaise, who provided us with keen eyes and an elegant touch, thank you for your support and contribution and for making us read so perfectly on paper.

The Co-Authors of *Catch Your Star*

Introduction

Congratulations! You have opened an incredible resource, packed with great ideas that can turn your life into a fulfilling, healthy and joyful adventure. You are about to discover how to *Catch Your Star.*

Personal development is much more than improving your talents. It is finding your identity and expanding your self-awareness, qualities and spirituality. It is a conscious pursuit of health, happiness and individual potential. It is building relationships with others and reaching out to offer your gifts.

With this book, you can discover proven ways to rise above those things which have held you back. You'll learn from amazing and inspiring individuals who have been through the process of improving their own lives and went on to help countless others enhance theirs. We have joined together to give you highly effective strategies that take you from where you are to where you want to be. Some bits of advice are repeated in different chapters—that tells you how important that advice is!

It's all here—how-to's for identifying your values and belief patterns, changing your mindset, and tapping into your dreams and intuition. You'll learn ways to find your life's purpose and discover your passion. You'll discover motivation for leaving fear and destructive patterns behind, and how to be a leader in your own life.

All the co-authors you will meet in this book want you to have quality strategies and confident know-how to pursue your dreams! We have shared our best tips and proven guidelines to achieve the life you may never have thought possible.

To get the most out of this book, we recommend that you read through it once, cover to cover. Then go back and follow the tips that apply to you, in the chapters most relevant to your current situation. Every improvement you make in yourself makes a difference in your life.

Your journey to a better you takes time, patience and determination. If you take action and apply the strategies, tips and tactics we share in these pages, you will reap many rewards. With our knowledge and your action, we are confident that you, too, will learn to *catch your star.*

To you and your continued success!

The Co-authors of *Catch Your Star*

Birthing Your Dreams

Start Your Journey Today and Keep Going

By Shontaye Hawkins, MBA

*F*ar too many people reach the end of their lives unfulfilled, unhappy and regretful. They regret not saying yes to their dreams. They regret not taking a chance. Birthing your dreams starts with a vision. Your vision becomes a reality by taking consistent action despite the perceived risks, challenges and obstacles. All you desire will unfold as you move forward and embrace the journey with trust, patience and perseverance. Be courageous, bold and committed to living your dreams and not living your fears. With the following nine elements, you'll be equipped, empowered and emerged in the life of your dreams. Welcome to the journey where life emerges and dreams are lived.

Vision

Vision can be summed up with three words—see, create and *live*. The life you see in your mind is the life you create. Ultimately, the future you perceive becomes the reality you live. Vision gives your dreams wings to fly. It is the heartbeat that excites, inspires and pulls you forward. Without vision, your dreams suffocate and remain submerged deep within. *I'll believe it when I see it,* is one statement that takes the life out of your dreams. A better statement is, *I will see it, create it and live it.*

Albert Einstein described imagination as "the preview of life's coming attractions." As women, we tend to put everyone else's dreams ahead of our own. Just as we nurture the dreams of others, the dreams that were placed in our hearts deserve to be nurtured, cared for and lived.

When I was training for my first half marathon, I visualized people clapping, cheering and smiling as I crossed the finish line. There were times when I would catch myself smiling as I visualized the crowd standing there, cheering. I held that vision in my heart and mind the entire 13.1 miles. Even when I was not sure if I could take another step, my vision kept me focused on crossing the finish line. Then, as I actually completed the half marathon, it was just as I had imagined. There stood countless people clapping, cheering and smiling as I crossed the finish line! It was the end of a race, however, it was the birth of a dream for me.

Your vision is not the end, it is the beginning of life.

Action

There are two forms of action—one gets results while the other comes complete with a full suite of sexy excuses. When you hit a bump in the road, it is not a sign to stop. It just means you must find a different path. If one does not exist, create it! Action defeats and silences fear, negative self-talk and doubt.

Focused, clear and consistent action yields results. If you stop, you have to start again, therefore do not quit. Keep going. One morning, on my way to a training run, I realized I had left my running watch behind. I felt very unsettled, even though I had run this path many times before. I had not realized how attached I was to my running watch. I decided to stick with my plan and run anyway. After about a minute, I saw the words, keep going written on the sidewalk in chalk. I smiled and kept running. A little while later, I saw those words again, *keep going*. I soon realized that in order to cross the finish line, I would have to be consistent and just keep going.

This is the same level of focus and consistency required to make your dreams a reality. Talking about your dreams is not the same as acting on them. Waiting for the perfect time is not taking action, either. There will always be a reason to wait. Focusing on your vision inspires you to take action. Feel free to cry, shout, crawl and scream when the journey gets uncomfortable—just do not give up. All champions have a scar or two.

Risks

When we do not know the *how,* we feel uncomfortable. It means we are entering unfamiliar territory. If everything you want is outside your comfort zone, then your comfort zone must be really uncomfortable, right? By definition, comfort is defined as content and undisturbed—at ease.

Therefore, one would think your comfort zone would be a place of total and absolute fulfillment. However, it is not because it causes you to settle for less and conform to the ordinary. There is nothing ordinary about living your dreams.

Risks involve embracing both challenges and opportunities equally. On the journey to birthing your dreams, you will discover that there are no failures. There are only opportunities and experiences that draw you closer to your destiny.

If you talk about living your dreams, yet you follow it up with all the reasons why you cannot start that business, write that book or ask for that promotion, then fear controls your comfort zone. Ultimately, it controls your life. Focus on your vision, not your fears. To hell with circumstances, take a chance!

Fear is the biggest dream killer of all. It paralyzes your mind and ultimately keeps you from taking chances. These chances push you through to your breakthrough. However, far too many people stop one step before their breakthrough. I believe one of the biggest dreamers of our time was Dr. Martin Luther King, Jr. He was willing to lose it all for the dream. Are you?

Trust

Just as God gave Noah instructions to build the ark, He provides guidance and direction for your dreams to emerge. There was no sign of rain when Noah built the ark. His trust was bigger than his current reality. His trust was in the vision. He was willing to let go of his plan to embrace God's instructions.

When the vision was planted in your heart, it came with everything required to make it a reality. To unlock the life of your dreams, be prepared to be tested. It is all a part of the process. These tests will determine whether you are playing Double Dutch with your dreams or if you trust the vision and the plan.

Often, we allow past challenges, disappointments and failures to affect what we believe is possible. Life is filled with experiences that teach and transform. Forgive yourself, release the judgment and do not be held hostage and enslaved to your past. It has no rights to your dreams. Trust is being blindfolded and handcuffed, yet listening to your heart and focusing on the vision despite your current circumstances.

If you are given instruction to take a step forward, do it. It does not require a certain number of "likes," "shares" and "retweets." When the dream was placed in your heart, it did not require anyone else to cosign for it. Others may not understand the dream and that is okay. It is yours to birth into the world, not theirs. (See Nora Cabrera's chapter, The Universe is Within You on page 33)

The instruction manual resides in your heart, not in the outside world. Are you willing to let go, take your hand off the wheel and believe in the unseen?

Courage

"I can't be afraid, it's my turn to be brave."
—**Author unknown**

It takes courage to face the giants of fear and doubt that show up on your journey toward living your dreams. Along the way, you can expect challenges, obstacles and a few dead ends. They are not signs for you to stop, they are opportunities to be fearless and create your own path.

We all fear something in life. The difference is how we each respond when we come face to face with our giant fear. Do you lean in and take a step forward or do you shrink back? Action is your secret weapon. With courage on your side, you are armed and dangerous— the strength, power and purpose of your dreams are bigger than your fears.

Taking action builds confidence. You may not see what steps two, three and four will be. However, when you take the first step and survive, you are empowered to take the next step, and the next. It all starts with a decision to be courageous and serve notice. (See Sonia Hassey's chapter, From Fear to Fearless on page 119)

Attention Fear: I'm sure you mean well, however your services are no longer necessary. We've added courage to our team and love the work they do. Thank you.

Patience

Patience does not mean that you stand still and do nothing. It means that you embrace every moment of the journey as your dream emerges. We live in such a fast-paced society that waiting for anything seems almost impossible. Birthing your dream is not a three-minute microwave dinner, it is a process. Sometimes the required work is internal, beginning with your mindset. Check in and see if your thoughts are in alignment with your dreams.

The most precious and amazing things take the longest to emerge. Take a diamond for example. It takes thousands of years of extreme heat, pressure and stress for diamonds to form. Changes in conditions, temperature and pressure can interrupt the diamond formation process and as a result a diamond can stop growing for a period of time.

Don't confuse patience with waiting. Patience is active. Waiting, on the other hand, is passive.

Desire

When I participate in running events, there are runners ahead of me, beside me and behind me, yet we all have one thing in common—a desire to finish. Some finish and some do not. Those of us who do finish, desire to cross the finish line more than we fear it.

Desire is that hunger deep down that does not go away with food. It is fed with a vision that inspires action, courage, faith and commitment. It is a love that truly lasts forever, not just until death do us part. It is that quiver, that movement in your stomach that lets you know that you are on the right path. It is a passion that burns deep inside.

Desire does not get lost like a set of car keys. I believe it is submerged in fear, guilt, shame, doubt and a whole host of other negative feelings and emotions. When you release these emotions, you find that your passion never left, it was always there waiting for you to make room for it to emerge.

Commitment

Are you interested in living your dreams or are you committed to living your dreams? There is a big difference.

Before you answer this question, be clear about what you are calling forth into your life. When you respond, *I'm committed,* you open your life up to shifts and change, some of which will come in the form of challenges and breakdowns. However, there is a gift that lies on the other side of breakdown—it is called *breakthrough.* As you move from breakthrough to breakthrough, situations will test you to see whether you are playing Double Dutch with your dreams or if you are fully committed.

Commitment says, *I'm going to live my dreams,* not, *I'm going to live my dreams if...* The latter is a negotiation between you and outside circumstances over which you have absolutely no control. On your journey, expect to be tested along the way, and most importantly expect to win! Challenges are gifts that help you discover how strong and powerful you really are.

I love how Law of Attraction expert John Assaraf explains the difference between being interested and being committed. He says, "If you're interested, you'll do what's convenient. If you're committed, you'll do whatever it takes." Think about Dr. Martin Luther King, Jr. and the sacrifices he made for his dream. He believed so deeply in the dream that he was willing to lose his life.

I do not know what you will face on your journey. I do know, however, that you cannot start pushing and then stop while your baby is in the birth canal. You are too close to your breakthrough to give up now. Own the dream. It is your baby.

Perseverance

No matter the conditions—rain, sleet, snow, hail or otherwise— your dream wants you to keep going. The conditions you face are no challenge when you tap into the power, strength and purpose of your dreams.

Nothing and no one can stop you except you. Too often, we look at our external conditions and then make decisions, versus looking inside ourselves for guidance and direction. Our external conditions will always give us reasons why we should not keep going. That is why you must remain focused on the vision and be consistent in your actions. When you lose sight of the vision and get distracted, doubt and fear find their way into your mind. It is in that moment that you decide if you are going to give in to your fears or if you are going to serve notice.

On the morning of my third half marathon, it was rainy and cold— very cold! This meant that I was facing more than two hours of cold, rainy weather if I wanted to cross the finish line. As I drove to the race, I prayed that the rain would stop. However, according to the weatherman it would rain all day. That was not the news I wanted to hear.

I stood in the corral with thousands of other runners, still praying for the rain to stop. No luck. There I was running in the rain, on purpose. At Mile One, a fellow runner handed me a small piece of paper with a scripture on it. It said, "Be sure of this, I am with you always, even to the end of the age," Matthew 28:20. I had been praying to God for a break in the rain. Instead of stopping the rain, He sent an angel to deliver a message that assured me that I could and would cross the finish line, no matter the weather conditions.

Are you willing to endure unfavorable conditions to live the dream? Do not stop now or you will have to start again. Just keep going.

Keep Going

> *"You've got to follow your passion.*
> *You've got to figure out what it is you love—who you really are.*
> *And have the courage to do that. I believe that the*
> *only courage anybody ever needs is the courage to*
> *follow your own dreams."*
> **—Oprah Winfrey, American media proprietor,**
> **talk show host, actress, producer, and philanthropist**

There was nothing in Oprah's past that told her she would be where she is today. More importantly, there is nothing in her past that she allowed to stop her from emerging and living her dreams. You have a dream waiting to emerge too. I encourage you to keep pushing, keep believing, keep dreaming and with all your strength and power, keep going. The perfect time is here and it is called *now*. It is your time!

Shontaye Hawkins, MBA
Emergence Success Solutions LLC
Unlocking Your Next Level

shontaye@emergencesuccess.com
www.emergencesuccess.com

Shontaye Hawkins, a business success coach and speaker, masterfully transforms the lives and businesses of entrepreneurs and business professionals. She encourages people to reach their full potential and build successful, more profitable businesses. Shontaye develops solid relationships with her clients, provides an exclusive, unmatched level of service and consistently drives bottom line results. Through her custom designed coaching and training programs, she provides winning solutions to define, create and unlock success in all areas of her clients' lives.

During her career with Fortune 500 companies such as Goldman Sachs® and Bank of New York®, she worked with top business leaders to build wealth in excess of $1 billion and attract high net worth clients. Now Shontaye helps entrepreneurs and business professionals create massive growth, profit and success in their own businesses.

As the CEO and Founder of Emergence Success Solutions, the premier coaching and training company, Shontaye inspires and empowers her clients to emerge and unlock their next level. Grab Your Free Audio Gift, *5 Critical Keys To Emerge, Thrive and Create Breakthrough Results in Your Business* at www.yourfreeaudiogift.com.

The Secret to Finding Your Bliss

By Linda Ballesteros

*H*ave you heard the phrase *Follow your bliss?* How can you follow something when you do not know what you are following? That is why I set out to first *find* my bliss.

Let's start with identifying what the word bliss really means. Bliss is when you are in harmony with your true self or your life's purpose. Your purpose is doing what you were born to do. Discovering your bliss creates a lifetime filled with meaning, joy, clarity and centeredness.

Finding your bliss allows you to access your powerful infinite potential. Tapping into your talents guides you to make decisions in your life not based on what is good or bad but rather on whether it supports your life's purpose or your blissful life.

> *"To be happy, one must find one's bliss."*
> **—Gloria Vanderbilt, American artist**
> **and fashion designer**

Do you sometimes feel that you are not living the life you dreamed of? Often, the decisions and choices we have made in life have taken us down a different road, leaving us scratching our head and wondering how we got here.

11

When you look around and hear of people who have the perfect job and are paid quite handsomely for their special gifts and talents, do you wonder why you are not one of those "lucky" ones? It is no wonder that many of us struggle unnecessarily because we have gotten things a bit out of order. We are encouraged to choose a career and then work at becoming an expert in that industry. Wouldn't it make more sense to discover your talent or what makes you happy and then learn how to make a good living and excel at it?

I have seen this approach show up in many aspects of my life. My mission in this chapter is to share with you some of the tools and techniques I used to turn my journey from a back road of potholes to a smooth highway. This is not to say that you will not encounter a few bumps here and there, however these strategies can ease your trip.

Look Within Yourself to Find Your Bliss

The first thing you need to know is that no matter where you are in life, it is never too late. It does not matter if you are a student, a mother or have raised your family and are now looking forward to retirement. It is never too late to find what you love to do and build a life around your talents. (See Sonia Hassey's chapter, From Fear to Fearless on page 119)

> *"It is never too late to be what you might have been."*
> **—George Eliot, 19th century English novelist**

The next thing I want to share with you is that the secret to finding your bliss is not in a book or outside yourself. The clues to your life's purpose and what makes your eyes light up are within you.

To find these clues, you will need to take a journey of self-discovery. Find the person you are and who you are meant to become. This journey introduces you to a new mindset which encourages you to create new habits.

You can use these as tools to help you avoid some of the potholes.

A Powerful Tool at Your Fingertips

The most powerful tool may seem simple and you actually have access to it right this very minute. I found that the use of affirmations have become the foundation to my blissful life. Anytime I find myself reverting back into an old mindset or pattern, I place more focus on affirmations. In fact, I learned how to super charge them, making a simple affirmation even more powerful and effective. This is the first step to shifting your mindset. It allows you to be open to receiving by changing old beliefs. (See Lauren Carbis' chapter, Inspire, Desire and Discover on page 97 and Tammy Phye's chapter, Tragedy to Thriving on page 129)

Shifting your belief starts with the words you use and the images you create daily. Using positive affirmations to saturate your mind with positive thoughts can change your life by eliminating negative images of your life. It has been proven that a thought must be repeated 180 times to be programmed. If you are talking to yourself day in and day out at a rate of 200 words per minute, how long do you think it would take to program a thought? With this in mind, it is important to keep your thoughts in check. Does your internal dialog support you and the life you want to create?

Consider your daily thoughts as a personal slideshow that repeats itself. The images on the slides represent your deepest beliefs. These images form your self-image which is who you believe you are and where you believe you are going.

> *"Thoughts become things. If you see it in your mind,*
> *you will hold it in your hand."*
> **—Bob Proctor, American motivational speaker**

You may have heard the statement *Thoughts become things.* It is true, however, if you are new to using affirmations, your belief muscle may be weak. Adding affirmations into your daily routine will strengthen the belief muscle. Try writing them on an index card and keeping it in your car. When you stop at a red light or arrive at a meeting early, take advantage of those few moments and read the affirmations out loud. Even if you do not see your affirmations working, have faith. Faith and belief keep the channels open for receiving.

Make the Law of Attraction Work for You

It is also important to stay excited about the process because positive emotions act as a gas pedal and accelerate the process. Your thoughts, emotions and even your goals have a certain vibration or frequency. The universal Law of Attraction is that you tend to attract similar vibrations. To find your blissful life you must be on the same frequency and same vibration as your goals before they appear.

Remember that
• What you notice
• What you give your attention to
• What you talk about and
• What you get all worked up over emotionally
is what you are inviting into your life. . . whether you mean to or not.

Open your mind to the clues to your life's purpose by noticing, giving attention to and talking about what you want to bring into your life and nothing else.

I must admit, however, there are times when it is difficult to believe your dreams could actually come true. Visualizing your blissful life can most certainly take you outside your comfort zone. Therefore, I created a transition statement to help give your subconscious mind a heads up that you now choose to create a new life.

Recite the transition statement as many times each day as you can remember to say it. Here is a transition statement for a successful business:

All of my past negative business building and income generating experiences are no longer true for me. In my new life, I have clients who seek me out and pay me very well for my services/products.

The transition statement can easily be customized for the area of your life on which you are currently focused, such as relationship, prosperity, personal and so on. You may even notice less resistance to blessings as they enter your life because you have already told your subconscious mind to expect changes.

We are constantly being given clues to finding our bliss, however we are not always in a place where we are ready to receive. The use of affirmations creates the mindset to help you to recognize and accept the path to your blissful life when you see it.

"Don't ask yourself what the world needs; ask yourself what makes you come alive. And then go and do that. Because what the world needs is people who have come alive."
—Howard Thurman, American philosopher

Search for What you Love

The next step is to explore and identify your passion. Each person has her own unique set of talents. As you search for what you love doing, you begin to see changes in your whole life. Your mood and your health improve.

My first experience with this happened when I found myself divorced from a twenty-year marriage. Those close to me attempted to encourage me by saying this was a time where I could do what I enjoyed, what I had passion for or always dreamed of doing. I have to admit, I had no clue what to do or what I wanted to do. After admitting that somewhere I lost myself, I made some decisions that changed the rest of my life. I knew that I had a responsibility to myself to get to know who I was and what I wanted to spend my energy doing. This led me on a journey searching for who I was meant to be.

I started by reviewing my life. This can be very scary and over-whelming, therefore I decided to take it in steps. Remembering what I was doing when I was 35, 25, 18, 15 and so on. Each revisit provided me with a few more pieces of information about myself. The most valuable information came when I went back to the age of five. One of the things I remembered was that as a very young girl, I loved to color. This was a love beyond just passing time. Therefore, I started taking art lessons and found that it came very easy to me. In fact, after taking lessons for one short year, I entered one of my paintings into a competition and won *Best of Show*. I even created a few special order pieces for payment.

Remembering something that gave me such joy was a clue to re-discovering a talent with which I was born. With this exercise, I learned that reconnecting with what I love is the recipe to finding my bliss.

"It's the repetition of affirmations that leads to belief. And once that belief becomes a deep conviction, things begin to happen."
—**Claude M. Bristol, American author of**
The Magic of Believing

The use of affirmations is designed to raise your vibration to attract that which is rightfully yours. If you spend time angry, fearful, worried, feeling lack and so on, you will not be able to attract and keep a life of love, joy and abundance.

There is a saying, *you cannot live the life of a victor if you live your life as a victim.*

Becoming more aware of negative feelings and thoughts helps you shed the role of being a victim and take on the responsibility for your life. This allows you to become the victor you were born to be.

Recapture Childhood Joy

When you start feeling the shift in your mindset, how do you manifest the elements of your blissful life into your life today? I found by tapping into the joy and the happiness I felt as a child, I attracted the opportunities that would bring those same feelings into my life. As a child you were not concerned by the label on the dress you wore to school or what society thought of your career choice. You were very much in touch with what made you happy and all decisions were made from a place of bliss. Getting back to that place awakens the talents you were born to enjoy and share with the world.

I found keeping a journal helpful in capturing the thoughts or feelings in the moment. Revisiting your notes from time to time proves to be a valuable resource as you continue to discover your talents.

Get clear on what living the life of your dreams looks and feels like. One way to state your desires is by using a visual tool like a vision board. This is a simple technique where you create a picture of what you want your future to look like. (See Nora Cabrera's chapter, The Universe Is Within You on page 33 and Jadwiga Pylak's chapter, Trust the Experience on page 159) Using poster board, magazines, images, powerful words or phrases and a little glue can be just what you need to see a snapshot of your future.

If you prefer a more technical version, there are computer software programs that turn your images into a movie with the music of your choice. Tapping into multiple senses makes this exercise more powerful.

Vision boards are very personal and I recommend that you be very selective about with whom you share yours.

Do not make light of your dreams. Treat them with honor and respect because they are who you are. Your dreams...your passions... your talents will lead you to your life's purpose.

> *"The future belongs to those who believe*
> *in the beauty of their dreams."*
> **—Eleanor Roosevelt, former First Lady of the United States,**
> **writer, humanitarian**

The process of finding my bliss has worked for me in other ways. For example, I recalled that as a small child, I loved to dance. My parents certainly did not have the money for formal dance lessons. Therefore, I often watched the TV show *American Bandstand* with my older sister. When her boyfriends would come to pick her up for a date, I insisted they first dance with me. To this day, I can remember what it felt like to be twirled and move to the beat of the music.

After my divorce, I re-discovered my love for dance and the desire to take dance lessons surfaced. It was all I had dreamed of and more. I could not believe how quickly I took to the steps and how easy it was for me even when others struggled. I met some amazing people and was having the time of my life when about six months into the lessons, I was surprised to discover that one of my regular dance partners was my soul mate. We have now been married for 14 wonderful years. Again, by doing what I loved as a child, I unknowingly was calling into my life the same joy and happiness I felt as a five-year-old.

I give much of the credit for the success I have experienced on my journey to finding my bliss to the power of affirmation. Using affirmations helps to raise my vibrations, allows me to get out of judgment and receive my blessings.

> *"By using positive affirmations, we can build confidence*
> *and get what we want out of life."*
> **—Charlene M. Proctor, PhD, American**
> **founder of The Goddess Network**

Now that you have an idea of how to find your bliss, you can start looking around for the clues that will help you discover your unique talents and passions. Just add a few of the tips, tools and techniques that worked for me and before you know it you will find that you can reach out, catch your star and live your blissful life.

Linda Ballesteros

linda@lindaballesteros.com
www.lindaballesteros.com

Linda Ballesteros inspires and empowers others to pursue their dreams and accomplish their goals. A renaissance woman, Linda is a former banker turned successful motivational speaker, business woman, coach and leader for women in business. She uses her positive energy to inspire, educate and motivate audiences. She delivers talks and presentations on issues such as business, dreams and goals, networking and marketing. Linda also motivates her community through speaking.

Linda founded Wine, Women and Wealth, a business women's networking group that grew to 400 members and merged with a nationwide organization where she served as the Texas regional director. With one-on-one coaching, Linda teaches women how to improve their businesses through networking, marketing and self-realization. She teaches women how to discover their divine song and dance that is uniquely theirs by tapping into their talents.

Linda empowers, inspires and teaches via her radio show, Power Talk with Linda Ballesteros, which airs on the Tough Talk Radio Network. Tune in Wednesdays at 9:00 p.m. CST to hear "ordinary people tell their extraordinary stories." Linda authored *Your Pot of Gold is a Handshake Away—A Step By Step Plan To Quickly Grow Your Business Through Referrals.*

Discovering Your WOW

The Power of a Women's Circle

By Maggie Schreiber, CDC

*T*he time has come for you to catch your star and to allow the brilliance of who you are to shine. I am honored to support you in creating a WOW life that is balanced, joyful and fulfilled.

One way to ensure your WOW life that I have seen work wonders for myself, my clients and the women in my community is to surround yourself with people who believe in you and act as a mirror of love and light, reflecting the truth of who you are. This might seem impossible if the people in your life are not this way. That is why in this chapter I am going to share with you how to find or create a community of like-minded women in which your differences are neither hidden nor illuminated, where there is peace in the sense of belonging.

You may wonder how you can achieve that when you feel overwhelmed, exhausted and empty as a result of an overbooked schedule, life transitions and the demands of everyday life, leaving little time for fostering friendships and heart-centered connections. The desire to connect with friends and a community is there, yet you may not have the energy to create an opportunity to connect in person.

I have found that social media is the next best thing to being there. A study done by Rebtel, a telecommunications company, found that 68 percent of the women surveyed reported they use social media to connect with friends. It is encouraging that we have not given in completely to exhaustion and busy schedules and have found a way to connect through the Internet.

I am someone who resists social media because I love connecting in person. I nurture and inspire clients to know they matter and their goals and dreams matter. I am passionate about their dreams and support them with creative solutions for making their dreams come true so they may live a more balanced, joyful, fulfilled, life. I coach them in a ten-step process, and through workshops and retreats. I am about connecting from the heart and in person. This motivated me to create a monthly gathering of like-minded women.

What if you could be part of a monthly community of women which encourages you to simply show up, be magnificent and connect in an authentic way, where you can feel nurtured and rejuvenated? When two or more women gather in a safe and sacred space of connection, inspiration, celebration and expansion, new possibilities appear, lives change and miracles happen.

As I was designing the format for my group called Women Of Wonder, I was concerned if women would take time out of their busy lives to join me. Could my instincts about women wanting to connect in a way other than through their computers be totally off base? Then I was inspired by a photo of the Osani Circle Game played by Efé children of Zaire Africa. The photo shows 22 children sitting in a circle on the grass, legs stretched out in front of them and feet touching, all connected.

I was intrigued and moved by the example of connection and the beauty of the circle. Belgian anthropologist and humanitarian Jean-

Pierre Hallet took the photo because he was amazed by the way children played and the story it told about their community. You can view and purchase this photo at www.connectingthedots.com.

The power of this circle eased my concerns of moving forward with a live-and-in-person monthly gathering and I saw this photo as a sign. As you consider starting something, know that anxiousness is natural. It is a common characteristic of trying something new.

At our first gathering, we had 33 women attend. Two years later, we averaged 35 to 40 per month. Hooray, women did want that personal connection!

Welcome to the community of Women Of Wonder (WOW). My intention is to share the value of participating in a community that connects from the heart, inspires dreams, celebrates friendship and expands joy. You can apply these strategies to create a more balanced yet, abundant, life with a group or gathering of your own. With a community you feel a part of, catching your star will be so much more possible.

Women Of Wonder S.H.I.N.E.

My background in event planning motivated me to create a gathering to grow into a community. Another way to look at it is, a party with a purpose.

> *"There are two ways of spreading light; to be the candle or the mirror that reflects it."*
> **—Edith Wharton, American novelist**

The beauty of WOW is that it follows a simple, five-step process that generates trust and allows for consistency and ease. The system is called SHINE, because when like-minded women come together in a sacred space and connect, inspire and celebrate, it allows their light to **SHINE**. Apply the SHINE principal when creating your gathering.

S is for Sacred Space. We create a sacred space with a candle-lighting ritual which sets the intention for the evening. A ritual takes something that is ordinary and makes it extraordinary, inviting us to consciously open to the sacred.

H is for Heart. We connect and open our hearts with a special meditation, allowing us to be more open, vulnerable and receiving.

I is for Inspiration. The topic of the month is what we as women wonder about. We invite a guest presenter to share her special blessing, passion or business. For example, essential oils (see Tammy Phye's chapter, Tragedy to Thriving on page 129), healing, stepping into your power (see Bev Adamo's chapter, Women and Power on page 191) and dream interpretation (see Jean Kathryn Carlson's chapter, Let Your Dream Speak on page 53).

N is for Nurturing. Different members volunteer to bring delicious, healthful food. As a result of being nourished and supported, we have a sense of value, joy and appreciation. We are honored and cared for.

E is for Express. The feedback I have received facilitating events is that women love to share their wisdom and learn from each other. We have created a space for women to express themselves.

The SHINE system has contributed to the success of the WOW community. I share it with you as a framework to create your own community. It allows you to connect from the heart, inspire dreams, celebrate friendship and expand joy in a way that is unique to your very special group. Here is how these elements allow you to create a life of abundance, balance and joy.

Connect from Your Heart

The power of a circle is that it allows you to experience connection face to face and heart to heart in wholeness and unity. By opening up to your heart connection through ritual and meditation, you experience compassion, gratitude and love.

Brene' Brown PhD, LMSW American author and Research Professor at the University of Houston defines connection as, "The energy that exists between people when they feel seen, heard and valued; when they can give and receive without judgment; and when they derive sustenance and strength from the relationship." She highlights her study on vulnerability and connection in her Ted Talk, *The Power of Vulnerability,* in which she expresses that to establish a deep heart connection, you must be willing to remove your shields of perfection and protection to be seen. Communities like WOW create the space for women to do that.

> *"The best way to lead people into the future is to connect with them deeply in the present."*
> **—James Kouzes, executive educator and American author and Barry Posner, professor of leadership and American author**

Until you have your own group or when you are away from your group, how do you connect from your heart outside a powerful circle?

• Set an intention to do something you love each day. Something as simple as sitting outside for ten minutes with the sun on your face, reading a joke a day or listening to your favorite song.

• Allow yourself to receive acknowledgements and compliments. My friend Lynn pretends her heart is a little mailbox—like the kind you made in school for Valentine's Day—in which she places messages for safe keeping.

- Through daily meditation, create a routine of opening your heart. I recommend a two-and-half minute sounding meditation by my spiritual counselor, Lynn Bieber. You can download this meditation for yourself as our gift to you at www.wow-womenofwonder.com.

Inspire Dreams

The key to making your dreams come true is to become clear about your dream, believe in it because it matters and take action to make it happen. One of my favorite things about Women Of Wonder is the fact that each month we are able to shine the spotlight on a dreamer and support her as she shares her blessing with the community. I am excited by the fact that through her dream, she can ignite the passion and dreams of the women in the circle. The best, most brilliant way to catch your star is to create a circle of women and support them all to catch theirs. You will be amazed by the power of the circle and what dreams are discovered and achieved. (see Laurie Leinwand's chapter, Making Friends with Change on page 73)

Recently, my friend and a member of WOW, Donna Maria Bedford, business coach, trainer and founder of Bedford Growth Strategies shared this about her experience at WOW...

"Women Of Wonder was the perfect place to give birth to my dream of my upcoming retreats, 'How to Discover and Unleash Your Passionate Inner Italian—Whether You're Italian or Not!' The Italian phrase for giving birth is 'dare a la luce' and the literal translation is 'to give to the light.' Women of Wonder provides a space that is filled with light, joy and enthusiastic support—an ideal place to give birth to the dreams that are a reflection of one's soul."

Donna was inspired to connect with her dream and ignited the dream of many of the women who want to visit Italy. So much that we have set the intention to manifest *WOW does Italy.* Imagine what dreams will come from the magic of your circle. Those dreams that will be birthed and filled with light.

What have you wanted to manifest in your life that is just waiting to be illuminated? For you to make this dream come true, it is important to initiate the first two steps of the Dream Coach® process, Intention and Integrity. These are the core building blocks to manifestation. Intention is what you want, it is the rudder that steers your life. Integrity is about keeping your agreements, telling the truth, and completing tasks. It is about being whole. Without integrity, intention is just a lovely thought.

For you to manifest a big dream, you must take risks. To take risks, you must trust yourself and nothing will promote or erode self-trust more than your inability to keep your agreements. The more you are in integrity with yourself and others the more you will manifest in your life.

"Every great dream begins with a dreamer.
Always remember, you have within you the strength, the patience,
and the passion to reach for the stars to change the world."
—Harriet Tubman, African-American abolitionist
and humanitarian

Until you have your own group or when you are away from your group, how do you inspire your dream outside a powerful circle?

- Create a sacred space by lighting a candle and setting the intention to meet your dreamer. Close your eyes put your hands on your heart and take three deep breaths. Invite your dreamer, the part of you that holds your dreams so dear, to stand in front of you and ask this question: *If time and money were not an issue what dreams do you have for me?*
- Hear from your dreamer, let your dreamer speak. Then write whatever comes, without judgment, criticism, doubts or editing!

If you experience those limiting thoughts, thank them for sharing and say to yourself *I am ready to hear from my dreamer.* You may connect to a dream that has been tucked away in a special box that is ready to be unwrapped.

- It may be a challenge to hear from your dreamer because you can become steeped in reality and forget how to dream. If this happens, I encourage you to start with the idea that *your dream is to discover a new dream.*

Celebrate Friendship

Friends are the angels that surround you with strength, make you laugh when you cannot see the humor in things, talk you off the ledge in the face of crises and remind you that you are loveable and love. The gift of friendship is something I appreciate. In WOW, women embrace your growth and expansion and walk with you on your path of everyday life to your magnificence. In their presence, you can catch your star and open to the brilliance of who you are. I started this journey as a way to honor those women who were blessings in my life. The group that you create will be a garden for friendships to grow, as I have seen with WOW.

"A good friend is a connection to life—a tie to the past, a road to the future, the key to sanity in a totally insane world."
—Lois Wyse, American author

Until you have your own group or when you are away from your group, how do you celebrate friendship outside a powerful circle?

- Take time to honor and appreciate your friends. Send an email with a friendship quote to express your appreciation. Use books and the Internet for resources.
- Purchase *Simple Abundance, A Daybook of Comfort and Joy* by Sarah Ban Breathnach, Grand Central Publishing, 2009. Read it

simultaneously with your friends and then connect each week with them and share your insights.

• Mail or drop off a little "unbirthday" gift to brighten their day.

Expand Joy

When like-minded women come together in a safe and sacred space that is connected, inspired and celebrated, the end result is the expansion of joy. I think about how many women I know who feel as I described in the beginning of this chapter—overwhelmed, exhausted and empty. The circle is the container that creates the space for joy to expand. During this time you give yourself permission to be nurtured and inspired. You fill your lamp with oil which allows you to stay healthy and heal your mind, body and spirit. This is the power of the circle.

> *"Joy is unlimited because each shining thought of love*
> *extends its being and creates more of itself."*
> —***A Course in Miracles,*** **a non-secular self-study course**

Until you have your own group or when you are away from your group, how do you expand joy outside a powerful circle?

Follow this three step **WOW:**

• Be **Willing** to ask for help. It allows you to be vulnerable and to connect at a deeper level.

• Be **Open** to receiving. You may be a giver, yet block the joy by not receiving.

• Be **Welcoming** of the gifts and celebrate with gratitude. The practice of gratitude helps you to focus on the joy, which attracts more of the same.

Expanding Women Of Wonder is my passion and dream. You can experience love, healing, laughter and wisdom as it radiates from your small circle, out into the world. We have witnessed women's lives transform and dreams come true. If we can do this one woman and one month at a time, just imagine the shift in the World to balance, abundance and joy.

Congratulations, you are now an honorary member of Women Of Wonder. You have learned how a circle of women radiates a heart connection through the sharing of a dream. You have learned how celebrating friendship in a safe and sacred space contributes to the expansion of joy.

I encourage you to adopt the aspects of Women Of Wonder and use the tips and exercises to experience a heart connection daily, meet your dreamer, celebrate your friends, expand joy with WOW, ask for help, receive and express gratitude. May you be inspired to join a circle of like-minded women or create your own.

Maggie Schreiber
Certified Dream Coach®
Founder of Women Of Wonder

925-212-2468
womenofwonder@comcast.net
www.wow-womenofwonder.com

Maggie Schreiber captivates audiences with her vibrant, approachable style. She connects with the audience at a heart level inspiring dreams and transforming lives. Her creative talks engage audiences, delivering insightful and compassionate solutions to overbooked schedules, life transitions, empty nests, and forgotten dreams, acting as a catalyst to creating abundant, balanced and joyful lives.

Maggie spent the first half of her career in dentistry as a registered dental assistant and office manager. She discovered her ability to nurture patients who were in pain and fear, and help realize their dream of a beautiful smile. Maggie eventually wanted a more creative way to serve others. Her life changed when she attended a workshop and discovered that who she is and what she does matters.

Maggie is a Certified Dream Coach® and a member of the Founders Circle for Million Dreams™ Campaign. She facilitates workshops and hosts weekend retreats. Her dream is to own a retreat space that nurtures and inspires women to know they matter. Contact Maggie for support in starting your own powerful circle or to explore ways to make your dreams come true. Download your free meditation gift at www.wow-womenofwonder.com.

The Universe Is Within You

Discover Who You Are Not and Let Your Truth Blossom Naturally

By Nora Cabrera

In today's world, we are surrounded and seemingly supported by messages that ask us to be true to ourselves, to live our purpose, to choose to be happy and rich. At the same time, we are equally bombarded with messages that we are not enough, that we need the latest and greatest and that we need less fat and more fashion. We receive messages that make us less accepting of ourselves and that we need to improve and take on more challenges.

This ends up creating what I call the *hamster wheel effect*—lots of running and doing with a deep fear of not going anywhere. There certainly is not much joy, freedom and enthusiasm in this hamster wheel. There is only a lot of stress, self criticism and the profound experience of feeling stuck—*secretly.* We do this secretly because we sure better show the world how great we're "doing" life.

What about that deep sense of purpose you have? The one that is quietly whispering in your ear every day that you are here to do something meaningful, that you are meant to experience life joyfully, living your purpose? You look at your life and think about it constantly. Then you hear the whisper. And suddenly, BAM! You're stuck. How the heck do you get from where you are at to where you want to be? *How? How? How?* If only it were as easy as running to the Life Purpose store and purchasing the map with your name on it!

Here's the kicker: *you* are the map! Everything you need to know to live your life deeply and with purpose is within you. (See Shontaye Hawkin's chapter, Birthing Your Dreams on page 1) This is not a matter of looking outside yourself to figure out who you are. This is a wonderfully rich, amazing honest, loving journey of letting the truth of who you already are—at your deepest essence—*unfold*. You are who you have been searching for all this time. You are the one who holds all the answers and you are the one who loves you unconditionally. Are you ready to step into that awareness?

> *"The call to complete ourselves brings a realization that we have delayed living the essence of who we are."*
> **—Marv Hiles, American author**

There is so much out there in the world in terms of the "doing." I call it formula living. It's an epidemic of formula plus fear. Do A plus B and you will get C! However, does that really happen? How many times have you jumped from formula to formula and either do not get the results you are looking for or get the results, and still feel like something is profoundly missing. I believe that we are moving out of that linear formula we "try" to live our lives by that focuses on results: once I get "C" then I will be happy, and so on. This is another way of living toward a future that has not happened and of not living fully in the moment. We are meant to live life in the moment. One moment at a time is all we have. Living fully present in each moment *is* living life! And life is fulfilling if we are present in the moment. (see Paula-Jo Husack's chapter, Lead Life Now...Not Tomorrow on page 179)

What is the secret to living this life fully, to living your purpose, to catching your star? There is no secret. There is no formula. You are already a beautiful, magnificent, perfect expression of you in this moment. There is nothing to do or become. You are already you. You are infinite.

You do not believe me? I get it. You still want answers. A path to follow. Someone to guide you. Yes, it is okay to still want those things. One day though, you will fully embrace the truth of who you are and all the formulas, tools, and everything else will simply fall away because in that moment you will know and none of this will be needed any longer.

> *"Let go or be dragged."*
> —**Zen proverb**

I will share that my particular path to this point was not an intense, life-altering spiritual event or a near-death experience or anything instantaneous or extreme. It was a slow and steady journey to my own unfolding and it happened through my work to get to know my "not-self" aspect. The "not-self" is strangely enough the part of yourself that you really think is you. Is your cognitive mind already going crazy? I fully understand that feeling.

When I first realized there was no formula, I freaked out. If there's no formula, then there is no guarantee and that is really, really scary to the mind. Your soul, on the other hand, is jumping up and down with joy! Take a moment to take a few deep breaths in and out through your nose and take in the following statement until you can feel it, moving past your mind trying to understand it:

You are not who you think you are or who you are trying to be, or even who others think you are. Your truth, your essence, lies beyond what your mind is trying to figure out, control and define you to be. Begin to let go and be. You are everything.

How do you begin to let go? I want to openly share with you the parts of my path that have had the most impact on my journey. These are not "steps." Each piece informs the whole you and there is no formula! Do not get caught up in the "right" way to go about the business of finding yourself or your purpose. Creation, nature, life, everything is spherical, not linear, and everything is naturally unfolding as it should. Choose what makes your heart sing and follow that unfolding. Then, when the time is right for you, you will move into another aspect and explore your unfolding through that. There is no "right" path. You are the path!

> *"Teachers open the door, but you must enter by yourself."*
> **—Chinese proverb**

Release Beliefs

What are beliefs? Beliefs are nothing more than *interpretations* you have attached to events you have experienced. It is that simple. Once you are consciously aware of the connection, you can choose to let go of the beliefs that are limiting you. I would like to share one of my limiting beliefs that affected me my whole life until I recognized it and let it go.

Back in 1986, I was a very happy and excited twelve-year-old, anxiously awaiting the launch of the Challenger space shuttle. For months, we had talked about how amazing this event was going to be—a *woman* who was a wife, a mom and a teacher was now going to fulfill her dream of becoming an astronaut and flying into space. As a young, impressionable girl, this was a *huge* message—we can have it all in life. Wow, how wonderful! And then on that fateful morning of January 26, 1986, we were all assembled into the school library to watch the launch. Seventy-six seconds into the launch, I watched in horror as the Challenger exploded in the sky.

At that exact moment, I formed an interpretation of the event that subconsciously affected me for the next 27 years of my life: I cannot have it all. I believed that if I chose to follow my dreams, I would die and abandon my family and loved ones. Can you imagine how that belief has affected all my experiences, decisions and paths in life? I have self-sabotaged time and time again when it has come to my dreams and my success. It is a no-brainer when you have to choose between death and the pursuit of dreams with success.

I was not aware of this until I was working with my life and business coach. Now I recognize that those moments when I am about to cross the line into something new, a new level of success, that feeling of contraction, fear and death can no longer hold me. I recognize it, bless it for trying to protect me, and step across that threshold. I do not die or leave my family.

Beliefs are very powerful—especially if you are not aware, not conscious, of how they shape your choices, views of the world and fears. They are boxes that you think keep you safe, yet they are actually prisons. It is time to do the work to let them go. Step out of the box and set yourself free.

Understand Projection

This is another *big* one! It is something you are unaware of...until you are. You project your "stuff" onto others and the flip side of that is everyone else projects their emotions, expectations and so on onto you. Therefore, you take on everyone else's projections constantly and have done this your whole life. You take on what someone says about you and subconsciously look for things that verify that statement.

For example, I grew up an only child and heard from various family members that because I was an only child, I was "spoiled." I never questioned whether or not it was true—never! I just assumed it was and looked for ways to fight against it. If I had just asked myself if it was true for me, I would have saved myself a lot of heartache! Those family members were just projecting onto me their judgments, jealousies and assumptions.

Experience Feelings

This is also a big one. We humans *love* our emotions. We love them so much so that we tend to identify ourselves by them. I *am* happy. I *am* sad. I *am* angry. I *am* frustrated. I *am* depressed. How I feel is who I am.

Is how you feel really who you are? It is time to recognize that emotions are like flavors of ice cream for your soul's palate! Just because you eat chocolate ice cream does not mean that you suddenly start going around saying you are the chocolate ice cream. It is just something you are *experiencing*.

Before you become aware of your emotions, you feel an emotion and then look for a past story or create a new story to justify that feeling! For example, if one morning you wake up and feel depressed, you might automatically start working—really hard—to figure out *why* you feel depressed and look for reasons to justify the feeling.

If you constantly subconsciously look for ways to justify how you feel, how can you allow for new possibilities? Our minds always scour our past to justify our present situation. If your present moment determines your future, where do you think you are headed?

The Power of Your Vision

Your vision matters. It is powerful! This is very important. It is one of my favorite topics. Do you have a clear vision?

Are you so busy talking about where you came from, everything that has happened to you and how things are right now that there is no room for the future? Are you in victim mode and do not even realize it? Do you blame everyone else for whatever is going wrong in your life or why you cannot be happy? How can your spirit, mind and body know where to focus their energies if you do not have a clear vision for your future?

Our minds actually respond strongly to metaphors and stories. What story do you tell yourself every day? Is it playing on a repeat loop? It is important and profound work to craft your new story and your vision. Start today. Write a new story for yourself. Create your vision board, a tool to help you get clear and identify on a symbolic level your desires and goals in life. (See Linda Ballesteros' chapter, The Secret to Finding Your Bliss on page 11 and Jadwiga Pylak's chapter, Trust the Experience on page 159) You choose images to represent your vision and place them on a board. If this is something you would like guidance on, please visit my website for more information on the Vision Board Quest Program.

Shifting Patterns

A valuable way to find answers to your circumstances from within is paradigm shifting.

The American Heritage Dictionary, 2001, defines paradigm as:
par·a·digm n.

1. One that serves as a pattern or model.

2. A set of assumptions, concepts, values and practices that constitutes a way of viewing reality for the community that shares them.

Most of us have lived our lives assuming that reality is what it is and we need to adapt to our current situations. If you do not like your current situation, find a way to get out or change it. *Paradigm shift: reality does not define you. You define your reality by your patterns and it follows behind you.* You are the energy that creates your reality. The days of looking outside yourself are over.

You will subconsciously recreate in your outer environment what is going on in your inner environment, within you. Your outer reality is just a mirror. If you do not like what you are experiencing, it is time to look within—with love, compassion and awareness. Once you shift within, your outer reality begins to follow.

This is why Feng Shui and even just clearing clutter are so powerful. Blocks in your physical environment—body and outer situations— are the big, blinking neon signs asking you to address things that are going on with you on a spiritual and emotional level.

"Our life is composed greatly from dreams, from the unconscious, and they must be brought into connection with action. They must be woven together."
—Anaïs Nin, French-born American author

Now is your time. If you think you need to be, should be and have to be in order to become *who you already are,* it is time to throw back the covers of all your beliefs, projections, fears and obligations. There is no searching for your truth and your purpose outside yourself. You already have all the answers within you!

Clarify your vision, polish your story going forward and seek out the guides and coaches who will help to place the tools of self discovery into your own hands and to gently point you in the direction of your own heart and destiny. Now is your time. Live your truth. Live your passion. Live your love—with courageous action.

I wish you blessings, courage, light and love!

Nora Cabrera

nora@noracabrera.com
www.noracabrera.com

Nora Cabrera is a visionary life and business coach who guides creatives and entrepreneurs to discover and fully live the true vision in their hearts while releasing the chains of fear and inaction. Nora's passion is helping creative entrepreneurs uncover their "whole truth" so that they may begin to make empowered decisions which in turn creates authentic joy and success.

Since 1989, Nora has been studying and practicing various healing modalities to facilitate healing, growth, conscious awareness and authentic manifestation. She believes we are ultimately responsible for our own lives and how we create what we experience. Nora says that without awareness and knowledge, there can be no wisdom nor courageous action. Nora grew up in Miami, Florida and currently lives in the Dallas/Forth Worth Metroplex with her husband, two sons and dogs, Lola and Yoda.

Nora's philosophy and practice is: embrace your authentic gifts and to step out into the world. Shift and facilitate healing and change within yourself and the world shifts and moves with you. We are all interconnected and part of the whole. Love yourself first to joyfully leap into the world with your gifts, living fully your purpose and true destiny!

Finding Your Voice

Expressing the Gift of Your "Song" to the World

By Jane Inch, CPCC, CDC

*W*hat exactly is your voice and what does it mean to find it? Today, we constantly communicate both directly and through a number of devices. Therefore, finding and knowing your voice has become increasingly important. Women have many choices and an online world 24 hours a day. Sometimes it is difficult to find our own unique voice in a sea of many. It can be a challenge to discover which activities and causes speak purely to us. We find ourselves making choices that feel like a "have to" or we choose what is expected of us. We often choose to do more of what we do not want, than what we do want.

When we have been on a life course or trajectory that has been laid out for us—or even by us—we go along with the motions before questioning our path. At midlife, many women "wake up" after raising kids and often feel disconnected, uncertain and unsure of their next step. They do not feel connected to their voice.

> *"There is no index of character so sure as the voice."*
> **—Benjamin Disraeli, former British Prime Minister**

Whether you like it or not, finding your voice is imperative if you want to be in business, in the non-profit sector or just be connected to the bigger conversation. Additionally, with all of the opportunities available to today's woman, it can make a difference to be strongly connected to your voice, and actually think about your own "personal brand" and what you stand for. (see Rebecca Gruyter's chapter, Stop Hiding and Shine! on page 211) What do you have to say to the world—in your words, in your voice?

I love working with women who want to do more with their lives. I love people who pioneer a new way of being and living. I have always been inspired by women who are leaders and mentors—those who want to make a difference. I love seeing people using their gifts and talents to make the world a better place. Women are launching businesses today that never even existed before—doing what they love! I believe we are all celebrities. That status is not just reserved for the few, we all get to catch our star and shine!

For as long as I can remember, I have been intrigued by voice. First, in its most elementary sense—the way it sounds, its different inflections, accents and tones. I can naturally impersonate those around me. I have always been fascinated by the different intricacies and sounds in everyone's voice.

In recent years, through my work as a personal development coach, I have become captivated by voice as an effective—or ineffective—communication tool. I notice when people become detached from their power while speaking, and when they do not seem grounded in who they truly are. As a longtime personal growth advocate, I am always curious about my relationship to voice and my understanding of its deeper meaning.

In 2009, I became absolutely taken with the *American Idol* rock star Adam Lambert. I will never forget the first time I heard his unbelievable voice echoing through the floor, as my husband watched him on the kitchen TV. I was busy creating a women's workshop in the office upstairs. I leapt up from my work and ran downstairs as fast as I could, yelling "Who is singing?" It had such a potent effect on me and it was inexplicable. His voice took me back to years gone by and made me curious about so much more.

"Words mean more than what is set down on paper. It takes the human voice to infuse them with deeper meaning."
—Maya Angelou, American author and poet

I did not know it then, however looking back I know this was the beginning of a realization that would pull a lot of questions together for me in seeking answers about what the voice means and why it is important to think about it. Singing is one manifestation of how we can use our voices and it illustrates the power it can have, physically and emotionally.

In what completely took me by surprise, I found myself, a middle-aged woman, attending a plethora of Adam's concerts. I was completely enamored by his showmanship, charisma and of course his unbelievable voice. I guess I was a groupie—along with thousands of other people of all ages who were in the same boat.

I wondered what it was about this artist that makes all these fans, many of them women, chase him around the world, night after night, city after city. When I returned from the last of 15 concerts, I had to extract what I had learned from this frivolous adventure. I needed to see why I had been intuitively and inexplicably drawn to this experience.

"The one thing that you have that nobody else has is you. Your voice, your mind, your story, your vision. So write and draw and build and play and dance and live as only you can.
—Neil Gaiman, English author

Male and female friends asked me what it was I was so drawn to in this nearly year-long period of my life. I had become part of the Adam "fandom." I needed to figure it out, because whenever I followed my intuition, even if it seemed *crazy*, I always learned and grew from it.

What I see in my day-to-day world can usually be applied to my work with clients. I often wove my own experiences and learning into the content of my workshops for women. Now, I sat down and put pen to paper and began to create the next workshop in my coaching business called *Reveal Your Inner Rock Star.*

What does this all have to do with voice? We all long to connect with others through our voice—which is most authentic if grounded in our values and guided by our vision. Intriguing celebrities like Adam Lambert do just that when they are in touch with their "voice" as they connect with their audience.

This parallels with women who seek more fulfillment in life. The voice of a singer actually became a perfect metaphor for my work. Here is what I learned from my experience going "on tour" with a rock star and being a part of a very intense and dedicated fandom:

- You have a song within you.
- You want to be seen and heard.
- You want to share your gifts with the world.
- You want to be resonant, current, and relevant with a message.
- You want to be a part of something bigger.
- You want to feel inspired and daring.
- You want to work your edge, whatever that looks like for you.
- You want to stay connected and happy. It's what keeps you young.
- Communications and social media are important for staying connected and, in many ways, youthful.
- We all want to sing our song to the world and have the world sing it back to us and reflect what it is that we stand for.

What Gets in the Way of Your True Voice?

Your mindset and self-talk. Your beliefs and messages about who you are can come from your parents, friends, culture, environment and of course, the media. (see Sonia Hassey's chapter, From Fear to Fearless on page 119) These messages become your inner dialogue and if you are not aware of it, you create your life from it. People tell themselves things they would not tell their own children, like *I'm so fat, I'm not good with numbers, I was bad today because I ate ice cream, or I will never make money as an artist.*

> *"If you hear a voice within you say*
> *'you cannot paint,' then by all means paint,*
> *and that voice will be silenced."*
> **—Vincent Van Gogh, Dutch post-impressionist painter**

Your self-talk is insidious and you may not realize it is operating in the background all the time. Without even knowing it, the messages you send yourself become your own internal goals and what you create in your life.

It is important to be the observer of this inner dialogue. Your internal dialogue is not who you are. You can change it, and cultivating awareness is the key to turning it around.

Setting impossible goals. Some of us think we need to be, do and have it all. We often end up feeling depleted and inadequate when we can not live up to our own unrealistic expectations.

Comparisons. I often challenge my clients to go on a *comparison cleanse.* Comparing yourself to others keeps you from recognizing your own innate gifts and desires. It prevents you from developing your own voice.

Perfectionism. The media's unhealthy obsession with youth and an unrealistic standard of beauty makes perfectionism all too common today. It does not serve you nor the greater good.

Saying yes when you mean no. Do you say yes to please others when you would rather decline? This fills up your plate and fatigues you. It also teaches you not to trust yourself. By doing the opposite of what you say, you are actually going against your own true voice. Cultivate awareness around when you say the opposite of what you mean.

Lack of clarity. When you are not connected with your values and highest priorities, it is difficult to make clear decisions and choose what is most meaningful for you.

Clutter in your environment. We often have clutter around us and clutter within. Clutter around you can be a bigger obstacle to getting things completed than you realize. Seeing clutter in your physical environment takes up space in your thoughts that can be channeled toward other things on which you would like to focus. Clutter in the mind includes all the thoughts of things you want to get done—again taking up real estate in the mind that could be better used for other meaningful pursuits. Having a "Clutter Clear Process" that works for you can be a valuable personal growth tool. It can move you closer to realizing your dreams. If you look at something in your home that does not make you happy, move it on and out to someone who will enjoy it! Many of my clients create a clutter corner by the door that is always being replenished with things they are not using and they can let go of—on to the thrift shop or consignment!

Eight Strategies for Finding Your Voice

1. Identify your values and live by them. Your values are ideals that breathe significance into your life. You can use them as a filter for all your decisions. It is important to identify and get clear about your core values. When you make decisions that align with your values, you move toward connection to your true voice. If you have not done it before, partner with someone who can assist you with identifying your core five to ten values.

2. Get in touch with what really lights you up. Discover your passions, purpose, gifts and talents. Pay close attention to what is calling you. What keeps coming up? Who do you want to serve? How do you want to express yourself? What makes you feel fulfilled? What do you see others doing that you secretly wish you could do too? Where do you hold back your true desires to avoid upsetting someone else? These are important questions to ask yourself.

3. Live intentionally. Notice your self-talk and live in awareness. Watch your inner dialogue. Shine the light on it and see it for what it is and notice where it may be holding you back.

4. Self-care practices. Adding regular practices of self care to your life is extremely important in the fast-paced world in which we live. Hiking, connecting with the outdoors, yoga, meditation and massage are only a few of the practices you can add in to your week to help you stay connected to your true essence. Make a list of self-care practices you would like to incorporate and add them to your calendar. Keep these appointments with yourself and you will be all the better for it...and for those around you too. (see Dr. Yvette Nadeau's chapter, Achieving Health and Vitality in Your Life on page 109)

5. Build a support network. Surround yourself with positive, uplifting and nurturing people who are moving in the direction you want to go. Be clear about who drains you and who does not. Eliminate the energy vampires in your life. You can feel it when people pull on your energy and do not bring you feelings of joy. (see Courtney Hawkins' chapter, Be a Leader—Live Your Passion! on page 201) Pay attention to your feelings and intuition about the people with whom you surround yourself.

6. Live with gratitude. Focus on the good. This key frame of mind brings more of what you are looking for into your life. Having a gratitude practice where you acknowledge five things each night that you are grateful for can be quite powerful. There are bright spots everywhere in our lives. Bringing them to the forefront keeps your mindset positive. It is from this place that we can attract more of what we love.

7. Connect with others. Take advantage of today's amazing opportunities for connecting both online and in person. Social media is a great way to discover and express who you are and to reveal your personal brand. Notice what you love and value and use it as an opportunity for personal growth and for serving others. Use your voice through social media to clarify your message to the world about what you believe is important. Practice with blogging and posting messages that reflect your values and passions. Share your interests and reveal your passions as you tell your story. Notice who interacts with you and who you connect with by being in alignment with your own unique brand and essence.

8. Move forward with a vision. Having an overall vision in your life is imperative. Consider creating a one-year, five-year and ten-year vision that brings your dreams into focus. Write down your vision, describing how you would like your life to look. Creating a vision book or collage with pictures, inspiring words and phrases can be a great visual representation tool.

With the eight steps in this chapter, you can pinpoint the intersection between your values and your vision, find your voice and catch your star!

Values ground you in your truth and a vision inspires you to move forward. From here, you can create and do the work in the world you are meant to do and connect with those who need you most.

It means being passionate about making a difference through what you have to say and what you believe. With so much information surrounding us, we need to be clear about what we stand for. Think about your own personal brand and how to best serve through it. Your voice becomes the instrument that allows your inner star to shine brightly as you express your gifts and sing to the world.

Jane Inch, CPCC, CDC
**Personal Development Coach and
Communications/Social Media Consultant
Reveal Your Inner Rock Star!**

jane@janeinch.com
www.janeinch.com

Jane Inch is a certified life coach, a communications and social media consultant and speaker. She empowers today's woman to create her next act with clarity, charisma and confidence. Jane offers workshops and one-on-one coaching for savvy midlife women ready to launch the next big thing in their lives. Jane makes personal growth hip, fun and relevant to modern, extraordinary women.

Jane is a Bay Area native and U.C. Berkeley graduate. She is a certified professional Co-Active Coach™ through the Coaches Training Institute™, graduate of the Co-Active Leadership program and a certified Dream Coach®. Jane is also a certified yoga instructor. She continually expands her expertise. She has been a member of Business Coach Ali Brown's Millionaire Protégé Club and has been coached personally by Marcia Wieder, coach to Jack Canfield and Founder of Dream University.

Jane has been extremely involved in fundraising for numerous Bay Area philanthropies. Jane loves hiking, skiing, yoga, traveling, new adventures and watching her grown sons play sports. She enjoys revealing her inner rock star at home with family and friends on serious karaoke nights!

Let Your Dream Speak

Are You Listening?

By Jean Kathryn Carlson, MA

What if creative solutions to your life's issues came to you free of charge every night in the form of dreams? What if the truth about who you are and hints about what to do next were whispered to you in your dreams? Would you listen? Dreams come every night to impart their view of what is really going on, offering elegant solutions to life's many challenges. Listening to my dreams over a span of three decades has informed, enhanced and inspired my life journey.

Every night dreams create a new, personalized drama in your dream theater. Imagine having to be in charge of coming up with a new dream storyline every night. Impossible! Yet every night, we experience just that. It is this highly creative quality of dreams that has kept me tuning in over the years. Each drama is unique, and each drama carries a customized message just for you. What might your dreams be telling you?

> *"A dream which is not interpreted*
> *is like a letter which is not read."*
> —*The Talmud,* **central text of Rabbinic Judaism**

Dreams Are Gifts

Dreams are mysterious gifts, wrapped in symbolic and metaphoric language, just waiting to be opened. Think about it—as humans, we spend about a third of our lives sleeping and a portion of that dreaming. It is astonishing that we experience the dream as if it were real and yet, upon awakening, we easily dismiss it by saying, "Oh, it was just a dream."

Dream gifts come in many different shapes and sizes. Some are long and some are mere fragments. Some have a decidedly other-worldly quality and some feel like they are simply rehashing daily residue. Yet each dream comes with many layers of meaning. Regardless of the topic or length, dreams always come with exact information needed for you to move forward.

Dreams are gifts that keep on giving. Their shelf life does not expire. Exploring either a childhood dream or last night's dream will reveal meaningful messages. This is because dreams are holographic, meaning they are like a multi dimensional view of our lives. They deal with the essence of who we are. Therefore, their messages are relevant no matter when we tune in. For example, about 21 years ago, I had the following dream:

Title: Crystal Appears. "There are two women on an icy island in the middle of a river. Another woman approaches from a wilderness area on the other side of the river. This wilderness woman walks through the cold, frigid water which seems surprisingly refreshing to her. As she steps up onto the icy island, she greets the other two women saying, 'Hello, my name is Crystal.'"

What was most compelling about this dream was Crystal. I was struck by her qualities. She was tall and thin—unlike me. She wore a flowing gown and moved gracefully through the water—unlike me.

She came alive for me and showed me those qualities. Through my focus on her in my imagination, she has remained very much alive within me. I call upon her when I am seeking clarity, seeking to be "crystal clear" about something. Crystal is as alive and relevant today as she was 21 years ago.

"You are not asked to figure anything out. You are not using your rational mind at all. Rather you are open to your sense of discovery. You are curious about who is visiting now..."
—Stephen Aizenstat, American psychologist, Pacifica Graduate Institute

Unwrap Dreams with Curiosity

All you need to begin working with your dreams is a sense of curiosity and a willingness to spend time with your dreams, allowing them to reveal their messages. When dreams are first remembered, even for the most experienced dream worker, a typical response is one of puzzlement. What could this possibly be about? Often, just being curious, relaxed and receptive to whatever comes will produce surprising results. For example, I recently had the following dream:

Title: The Toaster Is On Fire! "I put two slices of buttered bread in the toaster and walk away. I forget about it and when I return there are flames coming out of the toaster! I hurry over and lift the lever, blow the flames out and to my surprise, the bread is not charred. It is simply toasted to a light brown."

When I awoke from the dream, I was indeed curious about it. I asked myself, why is the bread already buttered? Why was it not charred to a crisp? I went on with my day and put the image on the back burner. Suddenly these words came to me: "How can I be on fire without being burned to a crisp?" This spontaneous insight gave me a chuckle and made perfect sense to me. I have experienced burnout twice in my life and have had concerns about burning out yet again. I have described that experience to others as being burnt to a crisp—the exact words that came in my insight!

Dream insights like that are often accompanied with an "aha," a sense of a "tingle" or "pop." The physical, visceral reaction in the form of tingling, goose bumps or other sensations accompanying these insights indicates that you are on the right track.

Every dream has multiple layers of meaning. It is not possible to exhaust the meanings dreams carry. Dreams live in the land of paradox. For example, flying in a dream might indicate high flying creativity, unbound by ordinary rules. On the other hand, it could also indicate that the dreamer is not grounded. It could even mean both. The beauty of dreams is that they move us beyond the world of either this or that and into the land of both this and that.

You can get started with your own dream work by recording your dreams and seeing what insights come. In the Practical Tips section at the end of this chapter, I suggest questions you can ask. Working with dreams on your own helps you become familiar with them, their themes and their symbols.

If you want to go deeper, consider joining a dream group. This reveals more layers of meaning because more people bring their diverse life experiences to the dream. More layers of meaning are revealed in the dream group process because each person in the group brings her own individual life experiences to the dream. It is like going to a movie with a few of your friends and having a conversation about it afterward. Each person has her own unique response to the movie. With dream groups, everyone hears a dream, imagines it as her own and shares her insights.

Since dreams are constantly breaking new ground for us, that is, they are at the cutting edge of our evolution, it is helpful to have multiple perspectives. I am not likely to see the deepest layer of meaning in my dream because it is still unconscious to me. It is crucial to remember that only the dreamer knows for sure what her own dream means. While an insight someone else shares is certainly valid for the one sharing it, only the dreamer can say for certain if that insight is valid for her as well.

Enjoy the Magical Landscape of Dreams

Strange things happen in dreams. The dream world is not bound to physical laws like gravity or moral laws. In dreams, for example, it is possible to fly like a bird or breathe underwater. The sense of time is completely different in dreams where past, present and future merge in a non-linear fashion. This can create a challenge when recording a dream because it is difficult to tell what happened first, second and so on. Often it seems as if events are happening simultaneously. From the waking life perspective, dreams are simply bizarre.

The imaginal realm of dreams is very much alive. At one level, everything in the dream is actually an aspect of yourself. Therefore, as you develop a relationship with the dream images, you are actually developing a relationship with one of your many inner parts. Using your imagination, you can interact with the dream and allow its images to come to life. For example, let us revisit the dream about Crystal. After recording the dream, I close my eyes and imagine the scene, opening my senses to everything there. I hear the sound of the river, feel the chill in the air, breathe in the scent of the pines wafting over from the wilderness area. Can I see her walking across the river? As I allow this dream to play in my mind, something surprising might happen. The ability to re-enter the dream and interact with images takes time to develop. Start wherever you are and be patient.

One dreamer shared a recurring nightmare that she had experienced for many years that included a menacing prison guard. As she opened up to the dream in her imagination, she was able to interact with the prison guard. She witnessed him morph into a more compassionate person. This changed the tone of the dream from fear to compassion.

Play Around with the Language of Dreams

Now you get to play word detective. Dreams love playful language. In my dream about Crystal, the word crystal plays a significant role in the dream. It is a woman's name and also refers to ice and rock crystals.

When recording your dreams, make note of names of people and places which might have another meaning. Might a dream about San Francisco be referring to Saint Francis? Also, watch out for all sorts of plays on words, like I or eye, bare or bear, sea or see, knows or nose. These may be clues to the dream's message.

In addition to watching for plays on words, be on the lookout for specific numbers which also might provide hints about the meaning of your dream. Is the number referring to an important year? A birthday? An anniversary? A year of significance in your life? Even if the number shows up in dollars and cents, like $17.76, it could refer to the year 1776. You may also add up the numbers and see if that number has significance, for example, $17.76 adds up to 21, a significant year in most of our lives. The numbers one and seven often refer to a sense of wholeness. The number two or a reference to two in the form of pairs of items can indicate a sense of duality. Be curious, let your mind wander and see what connections come. If you have a special interest in numbers, you could look up information about numerology on the web or at the library.

Dream symbol dictionaries give hints as to what a symbol means. However, I prefer to ponder the image on my own first. Your personal associations with the image are just as important. If, for example, you dream about a collie and your childhood pet was a collie, that association may be a key to the meaning of the dream. If you are interested in dream dictionaries, you might start with an online dream dictionary like www.dreammoods.com.

> *"What if every solution to every challenge*
> *is presenting itself in our nocturnal dreams?"*
> **—Peter Diamante, American writer**

Honor Dreams with Intention to Pay Attention

Honoring your dreams simply means paying attention by writing them down, thinking about them, enjoying them. This may sound strange, however, dreams seem to know if we are listening in or not. When you set an intention to honor your dreams, the dreams often respond with more dreams.

One of the reasons for my passion about dreams is that dreams present novel ideas that are simply not available to us in our normal conscious states. Dreams played a role in Elias Howe's invention of the sewing machine and Einstein said his entire career was a meditation on a dream he had as a teenager. It gives me hope to imagine that someone tonight might be dreaming of a solution to water shortage, world hunger or some other critical global issue.

Dreams have also played a key role in the literary world. Both Twilight and Frankenstein were inspired by dreams. Stephen King regularly turns to dreams for inspiration. I see my dreams as the most brilliant creative aspect of who I am, unfettered by inhibitions of any kind. If developing your creativity is calling you, look no further than your dreams.

Know that *All* Dreams Come in the Service of Health and Wholeness

This principle comes directly from the dream tool kit of Jeremy Taylor, one of my teachers. Every dream comes to serve your growth, your journey to greater health and wholeness. All dreams cited in this chapter are examples of this. Crystal has continued to point the way to clarity, ease and flow. The burning toaster is telling me about paradoxically living in passion without getting burned out.

Even nightmares, those heart pounding terrifying dreams follow this principle. Jeremy says, "Dreams come in the service of health and wholeness, *not comfort and convenience.*" Nightmares are nature's way of telling you there is a sense of urgency to a particular dream. Wake up and pay attention! I happen to love nightmares because right in the most terrifying part of the dream lies the most gold. Be sure to ask for help if your nightmares are simply too terrifying to enter alone.

I encourage you to continue tuning into your dreams. Record them or draw them. Dare to take a step into the wilderness of your dreams. Your life and your dreams can take on dimensions never yet imagined.

Practical Tips for Getting Started with Your Dreams

1. Purchase a dream journal. Choose one that feels good to you, with or without lines. I prefer blank pages so that I can draw or doodle and not be confined by lines.

2. Put your journal next to your bed along with pen or pencil. This simple step will help you remember your dreams.

3. Record your dream. Remember, a dream not written down or shared is likely a dream forgotten. Even writing key words helps you recall the dream at a later time.

4. Record the dream in the present tense. For example, *I drive up the mountain road.*

5. Ask questions. What is the feeling or tone? Who is in the dream? Do I know the people in the dream? Where does the dream take place? If there is a house, a car or other object in the dream, is it familiar to me? Are there any confusing points in the dream?

6. Let the dream simmer on the back burner of your mind. Certain activities, such as showering, gardening, walking in nature or rocking in a rocking chair help the mind to relax and allow insights to pop up. You might simply sit, be still and see what comes up.

7. Watch for synchronicities. As you go through your day, you might come across something that reminds you of your dream. A memory might pop up or something might come up in a conversation that connects in a surprising way. These spontaneous encounters can give hints as to what the dream is saying.

Jean Kathryn Carlson, MA
Let Your Dream Speak

415-721-7300
jk@wakeuptovibrantliving.com
www.wakeuptovibrantliving.com

With a successful background in education and educational sales, Jean Kathryn now enjoys the work of her dreams. Her enthusiasm for dreams and the inner life began in childhood. As founder of Wake Up To Vibrant Living, Inc., Jean Kathryn shares her passion through speaking, workshops and individual work.

An innovative life coach, Jean Kathryn uses several modalities like Emotional Freedom Technique, or Tapping, creative writing and collage to help clients listen to their dreams and make decisions toward a more abundant life. She is a certified Law of Attraction Coach® and a Dream Coach™ and holds a Dream Facilitator Certificate through the Marin Institute for Projective Dreamwork. Jean Kathryn studied DreamTending with Stephen Aizenstat in the six-month intensive offered at Pacifica Graduate Institute.

Jean Kathryn's rich inner life and abiding love of the sacred fuels her journey. She lives a delightful life in Northern California, enjoying hiking in the hills and savoring the beauty that surrounds her. Jean Kathyrn offers creative dream workshops and online dream group opportunities. Explore your dreams or other ways to work with her by emailing her at jk@wakeuptovibrantliving.com for a complimentary thirty-minute session.

Master the Art of Possibilities

How to Turn the Impossible to "I'm Possible"

By Tobey Allen, MA, LMFT-ATR

*W*hat do you think of when you hear the word *possibility?* Is it the mere potential of what you think is possible or is it an intention of what you know is possible? Having a mindset of an infinite amount of possibilities creates new pathways of seeing all your possibilities. We often do the same thing over and over and expect different results—this was Einstein's definition of insanity. If you change your perspective and realize there are infinite possibilities, you can go beyond your wildest expectations. You see phenomenal results.

There are many examples of how you can change your perspective. For instance, did you know that there are more than 250 ways to clean dishes? Virginia Satir, a brilliant family therapist, did a study on dishwashing and now the chore will never be the same. That's 250 possibilities!

Employees at Ideo®, a design and innovation consulting firm in Silicon Valley, brainstorm possibilities by plastering colored sticky notes on their wall. This process allows people to visualize their ideas. They move the notes around and team members vote on their favorite ideas or solutions. This narrows down the choices until they make a final decision. Brainstorming this way creates a plethora of possibilities!

I have spent years contemplating my possibilities and implementing the necessary changes in my life toward my goals. In this chapter, I want to share my wisdom with you. I have developed a unique strategy into the work I so cherish today. I am here to infuse the seeds of possibilities so you can grow in any direction your heart so desires.

"You do not need to know precisely what is happening, or exactly where it is all going. What you need is to recognize the possibilities and challenges offered by the present moment, and to embrace them with courage, faith and hope."
—**Thomas Merton, Anglo-American Catholic writer and mystic**

Catch Your Star Even When the Sky Feels Empty

As a child with a learning deficit, I felt I had to work harder to achieve the same results as my classmates. I was ridiculed for being the slow learner. The teasing was unkind and I sometimes felt isolated for being different. I spent a lot of time in my imagination. I suppose that became an asset because today it helps me think outside the box.

I had a goal of completing my bachelor's degree *some day*. I became discouraged about completing my education due to a math requirement necessary for transferring from a junior college to a four-year university.

One day, I received a pink slip when the software company where I worked was closing. I decided to go back to school to complete what I had started. However, the university stated it would not transfer me without completing the math requirement. However, if I tested positive for a learning disorder, I could be provisionally accepted into the school. Therefore, I did just that.

I took a critical thinking course and got my first A in college. Next, I had to complete the requirements for earning a degree in graphic design. The program director reviewed my portfolio and denied my admission because I could not draw a bobby pin to their specification. I found myself on a light rail train staring out the window, crying. My star faded and so did my dream—or did it? Within moments, a stranger approached me with comforting words, "Whatever it is, keep the perspective." I never forgot those words and I live by them this very day.

As it turns out, my mother, a retired special education teacher, suggested I go into art therapy—a wise suggestion, as I love art and psychology. I changed my major and went on to graduate school to get my master's degree in counseling and art therapy.

"It always seems impossible until it is done."
**—Nelson Mandela, South African anti-apartheid activist,
revolutionary, politician and humanitarian**

Change Your Perspective, Focus on the Possibilities

I often say to others that it is not the path on which we started, but the path on which we ended up that provides clues to how we have traveled in life. My story is about the many paths I have taken, often with forks in the road and detours, however I have somehow managed to find my way. How did I get to my destination? I got there by enjoying the journey along the way and by being open to all the possibilities that were presented to me. (see Lauren Carbis' chapter, Inspire, Desire and Discover on page 97 and Beverly Adamo's chapter, Women and Power on page 191)

How can you create all possibilities for yourself? By changing your perspective. If you are willing to focus, the answers become clear.

As an art therapist, if I want to change a color, all I have to do is open the jars of paint and the color appears. If the color I want is not available, I can mix the colors to specification. The universe is a lot like the paint set. When an option is not available, it is time to create a possibility. In the book *A Creative Companion,* by SARK, published by Celestial Arts in 2004, the author gives this example of changing your perspective to create the result you want.

Australian artist Ken Done created a painting and thought his work would look great if it were made into bed sheets. However, no one could see the vision he had of his product. When he took the idea to a sheet company, they did not understand his concept and turned him down. Ken did not give up. He changed his perspective and saw another possibility. He painted the image on a white bed sheet and presented it to the sheet company, which then placed an order. By making the vision real, he communicated in a way that the company could see his perspective. The fabulous sheets were a big hit and made it to the department stores.

"You must do the things you think you cannot do."
—Eleanor Roosevelt, former First Lady of the United States, writer, humanitarian

Adjust the Lens to See All Possibilities

Are you ready to make your vision real? I use the word FOCUS to develop a five-step strategy to help you hone in on what you desire.
Find the perspective
Open to your heart's intelligence
Clear your mind to create space
Universal laws—creative forces that guide you
Service gives purpose

Step 1: Find the Perspective

Prepare your lens for possibilities. Just as you need to adjust a camera lens to bring the desired picture into view, you can adjust the lens of any situation or desired outcome to see all the possibilities available to you. What you focus on expands. If your lens is dirty or smudged, you must first clean it. If your previous actions were unsuccessful, your lens may already be scratched. Do not worry, you can simply change your lens or point of view.

- Consider these questions: What possibilities would you like to create? What have you done so far to achieve the results? Describe your current lens—are you seeing what you want to see? Are there any limitations to your view or is your view blocked by someone else's projections of what they want you to see?
- Adjust your lens of possibilities. Try this exercise to find your trusted advisor of possibilities. Begin by finding a comfortable place to sit undisturbed. Close your eyes. Imagine you are looking through the viewfinder of a camera lens. This lens is crystal clear. It sees your possibilities for your given situation from a new perspective. Describe the sensation of having your dream fulfilled. What does it look like? Are there specific people who can help you? Imagine that you have just received advice from a trusted ally. What instructions, if any, does he or she give you toward your goal? Thank your advisor(s) for the information. Know that you can return to this inquiry any time you need advice. Now open your eyes.

Step 2: Open to Your Heart's Intelligence

Within the last two decades, neuroscientists have concluded that the human heart has its own independent nervous system, referred to as "the brain in the heart." Researchers at the Institute of HeartMath, led by Doc Childre, have established a comprehensive system that provides the framework for understanding how this intelligence works including information, tools and techniques to access the heart's wisdom.

To access your heart's intelligence now, simply breathe through your heart. Send loving thoughts to something or someone you appreciate. Next, send yourself these loving thoughts. To take it a step further, ask your heart's intelligence to give you a new perspective on any given situation. Ask your heart what the best outcome or solution would be. Write down the answer you received.

Step 3: Clear Your Mind to Create Space
When was the last time you gave your mind a break from all the monkey chatter throughout the day? According to the National Science Foundation, it is estimated that our brains produce as many as 12,000 to 50,000 thoughts per day depending on how deep a thinker you are. It is no wonder we are so overloaded.

Jon Kabat-Zinn founded the Mindfulness-Based Stress Reduction program at the University of Massachusetts. This ignited a growing interest and application of mindfulness ideas and practices worldwide. Mindfulness is valuable for creating wisdom and clear thinking. Emptying your mind leaves room for new ideas and possibilities!

Experience mindfulness now. Be the observer. Observe yourself in the moment while doing an activity. What do you notice? How is your body feeling? Is it relaxed or tense? Slow your pace and notice the details of that activity. Do you feel rushed or comfortable with the timing? Notice if your senses are heightened. When you have completed the activity, write down your experience. To take this exercise a step further, observe the details in a garden. Notice the veins on the leaves of the trees. Notice the bark on the trees. See the forms as a canvas painted by the universal creator.

Step 4: Universal Laws—Creative Forces that Guide You
Once you have changed your perspective, accessed your heart's intelligence and cleared the excessive chatter, you are ready to tap

into the many laws including the Law of Attraction. According to Bruce McArthur, who wrote *Your Life: Why It Is the Way It Is and What You Can Do About It,* published by A.R.E. Press in 2012, your life is governed by impartial and forgiving laws that are universal and divine in nature. When you tap into these laws, you can create unlimited possibilities to help solve difficult problems, reach a higher source of wisdom and create infinite abundance and joy!

The Law of Attraction, for example, says that you can become what you desire. The creative forces respond to the desires you hold in your mind as beliefs. By believing in your potential and doing what you love to do, you create a flow in the universe. In time, if you choose to do so, your desire can be supported as your life's work and the universe can support you in doing what you love to do.

Create a possibilities box. This magic box will hold your possibilities as a prayer box for all that you desire. Here is what you will need for this box.

- Cardboard box (sold unfinished in craft stores and are inexpensive)
- Decoupage medium (like Mod Podge®)
- Scissors
- Foam paint brush
- Magazines, scrap booking paper
- Optional—stickers, iridescent sparkle glaze (to give it a magic quality)

Find quiet time for reflection. Create a box that represents infinite possibilities using words and images. First, cut your images out of magazines. Next, paint the images in place with a foam brush and decoupage varnish. Decorate the inside as well. Then, write your possibilities on small slips of paper. Roll these into scrolls, tie them with string and place them in the box. When the varnish has dried, write *thank you* on each of the outside corner edges of the box. Inside, write *all that is in this box is so.*

Place your box in a sacred space in your home where it will not be disturbed. Be amazed at how setting the intention can attract possibilities!

Step 5: Service Gives Purpose and Possibilities
People often ask me, "How do I know my purpose?" My answer lies in being of service to others. By being passionate about living a life on purpose, you become who you are. Instead of living a life of never-ending doing, you can instead do what you do best—be a human being. More possibilities happen when you are of service.

Muhammad Yunus is a practical visionary. One day, he loaned $27 of his own money to 42 stool makers in a tiny village. This loan provided the raw materials for their business and helped them break the cycle of poverty for good. In his book *Banker to the Poor,* published by PublicAffairs in 2003, Muhammad details his journey of how he created a micro-lending bank to eradicate poverty in Bangladesh. Today his bank, Grameen®, has inspired more than 250 institutions in nearly 100 countries to create funding through micro-lending.

Turn your purpose into a possibility. Write down five ways you can provide service to others through living your purpose. Research five organizations related to your passion and expertise for which you could volunteer. Reach out to at least one with which you feel a connection. Know that your presence is their present. Your gifts are meant to be distributed to the world!

"With God, all things are possible."
—Matthew 19:26, *The Bible*, King James Version

Unlock Your Possibilities Now

Here are five fabulous key ideas to help you unlock your possibilities:
1. Start a journal of all possibilities. Write your possibilities on sticky

notes. Stick them onto a poster board so you can reposition them. Look in magazines for images and words that support your creative idea(s). You can create an intention board and glue these images down or if you prefer, keep them fluid allowing for repositioning by using double sided tape.

2. Throw a possibility party. Invite three or more friends and brainstorm and ask for clarity and perspective.

3. Give fuel to your ideas and launch your success! Blog, start a Meet-up Group, invite others to guide you or even join you on your venture using Internet crowd funding.

4. Make your possibilities real. If you have a design concept, print it using a 3D image printer. This way, your concept is tangible and you can more easily convey it to others.

5. Be amongst the meeting of minds and attend a Seeds of Possibilities workshop. You can also hire a Seeds of Possibilities Coach™ for a personalized assessment toward reaching your possibilities.

Infuse the seeds of possibilities and watch your vision grow. I encourage you to change your perspective with the five-step FOCUS strategy you learned in this chapter. Try some of these suggested keys to unlock a plethora of ideas. You may be surprised and amazed how you, too, can master the art of possibilities and turn the impossible into "I'm possible!"

Tobey Allen, MA, LMFT-ATR
Seeds of Possibilities Coaching, Inc.
I turn Impossibilities to Possibilities

925-289-9204
tobey@seedsofpossibilitiescoaching.com
www.seedsofpossibilitiescoaching.com

When Tobey Allen, founder of Seeds of Possibilities Coaching™, graduated from Notre Dame De Namur University, she discovered she had a gift for seeing beyond the ordinary to the extraordinary. Her keen sense of intuition and practical wisdom has brought her to various settings including hospitals, hospices and schools. Tobey has been helping both adults and children reach their full potential and create new possibilities for themselves since 2002.

Tobey has a master of arts degree in marriage and family therapy and is a registered clinical art therapist. She received her certification as an Integrative Medicine Practitioner at the Institute for Health and Healing at California Pacific Medical Center in San Francisco. Tobey's expertise includes art therapy, guided imagery and Mindfulness Based Stress Reduction™. She has facilitated HeartMath™ groups.

Tobey is a licensed marriage and family therapist. Her specialties include stress management and life transitions. She has worked with countless parents, teens and women entrepreneurs, showing them how to focus so they can achieve their goals. Tobey has emerged as a sought after speaker in showing how you can reach all possibilities and capture your star!

Making Friends with Change

Learning to Challenge Your Status Quo Triumphantly

By Laurie Leinwand, MA, LPC, CC

*M*aking a change in your life requires effort, energy and incredible persistence. Whether you perceive a change as monumental or of little consequence, it can ultimately have far-reaching effects. Without it, you remain exactly where you are today. People either live for change or struggle against it, resist it and vehemently avoid it. Change evokes powerful emotions ranging from intense fear and anxiety to excitement and pure exhilaration. It represents saying goodbye to the comfort of what is familiar and requires you to learn or expose yourself to something new.

Develop your capacity to befriend change and you open yourself to a world of possibility. Instead of feeling paralyzed, defeated or blindsided by change, you become less bound by fear, better able to adapt and more likely to capitalize on new opportunities.

Inertia is incredibly powerful, making it much easier to stay still and tolerate the status quo. This chapter will challenge you and provide you with tools to successfully embrace change. You will see change as the means to reach your goals and move your life forward. Welcome it and begin a journey marked by growth and expansion—and realize your dreams.

*"If you change the way you look at things,
the things you look at change."*
—**Wayne Dyer, American author and speaker**

I have not always been a fan of change. I like knowing what to expect and when to expect it. I appreciate feeling in control. However, within the last few years, I noticed I was lacking fulfillment, excitement and growth. I felt proud and excited for my children, however I was no longer doing much for myself. I was standing still and getting bored with it. My career had lost momentum. I was not making my marriage a priority, not in good shape, not making enough time for friends and simply not having enough fun.

Time was marching on and I was a spectator instead of a participant in my life. Yet, this was my story and I was in charge of writing it! I would have to either allow things to remain the same or make a conscious decision to create and embrace change. I chose the latter. In that small, simple step, my world and my power expanded greatly. Sometimes life forces you to adapt to change. However, change can also be implemented as a tool in creating the life you desire. I feared three things in connection with change: what I did not know, failing and embarrassment. I found that none of those things could destroy me. Change has become my safety net. When things are not working for me, I take it as a sign that I need to either change things in my world or change how I perceive them.

*"When we are no longer able to change a situation—we are
challenged to change ourselves."*
—**Viktor E. Frankl, Austrian psychiatrist and writer**

Prompting change has done a lot for me in the last few years. I have a new business that enables me to help more people. I now belong to a book club and read much more as a result. I see friends more often. I work with a personal trainer to get in shape. I step into fear by challenging myself regularly and learning from mistakes rather than beating myself up over them. I take responsibility for my own happiness. I no longer feel frustration or blame others. I am happier and the people surrounding me are too.

Embracing change has also impacted my clients. A client who hated her job so much it was causing her emotional and physical distress, kept waiting for the perfect time and circumstances to leave. Finally, she simply chose change. Without lining up her next job, she resigned. She suddenly, and perhaps ironically, felt in control again and was able to focus her efforts wholeheartedly on finding her next right opportunity. She received multiple job offers and chose the best option for her.

I am excited to share with you some key strategies to help you welcome change into *your* world.

See the Signs

The first step in inviting change begins with acknowledging you want more or better for yourself. Signs of this include lack of energy, less meaningful engagement with others, decreased motivation, boredom, having a short fuse, constant frustration and blaming others for your problems. These symptoms are powerful signals that you need to alter something in your life. Give yourself permission to do something about it, rather than allow the "blah-dom" to continue.

> *"For the past 33 years, I have looked in the mirror every morning and asked myself: 'If today were the last day of my life, would I want to do what I am about to do today?' And whenever the answer has been 'No' for too many days in a row, I know I need to change something."*
> —**Steve Jobs, American entrepreneur and inventor**

Recently, I realized I was tired and often felt lousy. I was not exercising regularly, rarely pushing myself beyond my traditional limits. My thoughts, emotions and physical unrest were a huge red flag. Something needed to change and I was responsible for making it happen.

Action Step: Determine whether you are experiencing three or more symptoms indicative of change.

Identify Exactly What You Want to Change

To figure out what you want to change, be as specific as possible. Saying you want to make more money or that you want your life to be more meaningful is not precise enough. If you simply enter a town and state into a GPS, you might end up somewhere near where you want to go, however it is unlikely you will reach your desired destination. Entering the specific street address saves you a lot of time, effort and frustration. Uncover the particulars of what you seek.

Words have power. Writing your intentions regarding change is a way for you to own what you want—a declaration. This written statement is your Commitment to Change. Visualize your words even when they are not right in front of you. Then you can talk about your quest for change with others, despite the hesitation or fear you may attach to it. Post your commitment prominently to ensure your day-to-day actions are in line with creating your specific change scenario. (see Erin Summ's chapter, Creating Powerful Goals to Catch Your Star on page 139)

You may have considered the pros and cons of making a significant change. There is *also* great value in contemplating the pros and cons of maintaining the status quo! This practice offers greater clarity. Notice the feelings that come up in connection with each of the pros and cons. These feelings serve as important clues about how to proceed.

Action Step: Write your Commitment to Change and post it prominently for regular viewing.

Try the Change on for Size

Picture your change having already been actualized. What impact will it have on you, the way you behave, the others in your world and how they respond to you? What else will change as a result? Will the change "fit"? This exercise provides you the opportunity to anticipate potential obstacles along your path and allows you to be more cognizant of what you need to do to pave the way for your success.

Action Step: Find a distraction-free zone to visualize the change you desire.

Set the Stage—Create a Space for Change

Lay the groundwork for your change to truly take hold. Lack of time, energy and money are three common reasons people settle for what they know, and retreat from what they truly want. Setting the stage often requires using each of those resources.

Your status quo came to exist over time, with lots of repetition. Those grooves run deep. Creating a *new* set of "tracks" takes conscious and frequent effort. Devote time to establishing a different way of doing things. Consider designating certain hours in your schedule for this purpose to guarantee your objective does not fall by the wayside. Getting enough sleep and eating healthy ups your energy levels and greatly facilitates your overall change process.

Money can promote change. Spending money involves cost, but so does not achieving what you want. (see Anne Kjellgren's chapter, Create Your Rapid Turnaround on page 85) Look at how you spend and see if you can discover ways to reallocate your funds. You might be surprised at what you find. Challenge the "no money" notion and determine if there is, in fact, something you can do to invest in yourself wisely.

Surround yourself with people who can offer encouragement and lift you up when you are discouraged, impatient and feel like giving up. Are you willing to receive support when someone offers it to you? Are you able to ask for it? Begin constructing your foundation of support if it is not already in place, and be sure that you are capable of accepting assistance from others. (see Maggie Shreiber's chapter, Discovering Your WOW on page 21)

A role model or mentor is an incredible resource. Learn from someone who has implemented a similar kind of transformation. Discover what your role model's experience was like with regard to making a change. What obstacles can he or she identify that you may not have considered? What steps did he or she take to overcome them?

Action Step: Name two things you can do to set the stage for change.

Create a Map

Once you figure out precisely what you want to change and set the stage, it is time to formulate an action plan. Map the steps and stages involved. Anticipate true obstacles and develop strategies for overcoming them.

Make your steps small, manageable and achievable to ensure a greater likelihood of success. Consider setting time limits to ensure you remain on track.

Remember to tap into resources available to you and modes of support that will reinforce your efforts. While developing your plan, consider again how others might react to the change and what needs to happen in order to maintain it—this is a crucial part of the plan.

> *"Change does not roll in on the wheels of inevitability,*
> *but comes through continuous struggle."*
> **—Martin Luther King, Jr., American clergyman,**
> **activist, Civil Rights leader**

Be prepared to measure and acknowledge your progress along your journey toward change. Appreciate what goes according to plan and what does not—those are rich opportunities for learning! Be grateful in other areas of your life. Thinking positively elevates your energy. Negativity depletes it, blocking you from noticing that which is working well, ultimately shutting you down. Reward progress and celebrate important milestones.

Action Step: Map out the first five small steps required to implement your change.

Eliminate Excuses and Identify Your True Obstacles

We use excuses to avoid discomfort. They have emotions such as guilt, shame or disappointment attached to them. Those feelings indicate it is time to part with your excuses!

Are you afraid of making mistakes? You can learn from your screw-ups—it would be a mistake not to have them! They can enrich your change process and teach you where not to waste your energy moving forward.

Do you blame others for not seeking change? Blaming others puts power in other people's hands. Figure out what *you* can do to affect your situation and create impact. Discover, and work within, your locus of control.

> *"You must be the change you wish to see in the world."*
> —**Mahatma Gandhi, Indian independence leader**

Do your obstacles include negative self-talk? For example, *Who do you think you are?* or *You couldn't possibly achieve that!* Examine your inner dialogue and replace some of those self-defeating messages with more encouraging ones like *I deserve happiness or I will be proud of myself if I do this.*

Naming your obstacles helps you develop strategies for overcoming them. It can minimize them and decrease the feelings of overwhelm associated with them.

Perseverance, your determination and your ability to push through that which is difficult, disappointing and tempts you to give up, determines how easily you embrace change. To navigate the rough patches, you must not only be *willing* to implement your plan, you must actually *do* it!

Do not succumb to excuses. My personal trainer did not show up for my first training session due to confusion with one of his other clients. I could have decided that he was unable to help me. I could have used his no-show as my excuse to not get fit, blaming him. However, I chose not to. He apologized, we rescheduled, and my journey to fitness began a couple of days later.

Action Step: List your obstacles and then cross out those that are actually mere excuses.

Face Fear and Combat Procrastination

Fear alone can prevent you from making friends with change. You may fear the unknown, the next step or even success. Be willing to step into the uneasiness in order to s-t-r-e-t-c-h. Think of the incredible possibilities that exist if you choose to face the fear.

Procrastination is often a way to avoid what you fear and serves to limit your choices. With limited choices, it is much easier to defer to the way things have always been. Instead, make efforts to plan and welcome change into your world. Set the stage and create your map. You do not need procrastination to be your default. Lean into your fear and sample the magic outside your comfort zone.

Focus on what you *can* do and what you want your change to look like. What you focus on grows. If you concentrate on what you dislike, it looms larger in your mind. Often the thing you fear most is the very thing you need to do right now in order to create your next chapter.

Action Step: Name the thing you fear most associated with change and prepare to face it.

Take Action

Embracing change is akin to the birth process. You sign yourself over to uncertainty, have faith all will turn out okay, believe in your ability to handle what will come next, experience physical pain, feel profound emotions and surrender to the process. There is little assurance that you are fully equipped or that everything will go according to plan.

Your journey to change is the process of giving birth to your future possibilities. Change is a necessary component of your growth, development, progress and experience. Change is critical to finding balance, fulfillment, meaning and happiness.

- Determine what needs challenging in your status quo right now.
- Go back through this chapter and implement each action step.
- S-t-r-e-t-c-h yourself and expand your world.

> *"If we don't change, we don't grow. If we don't grow,*
> *we aren't really living."*
> **—Gail Sheehy, American author**

The change you cultivate opens the door to creating your best life. Befriend it, plan for it and savor the experience.

Change rarely waits for a perfect time, place or set of circumstances. Your decision to seek it will be your catalyst. Begin your rewarding journey toward change. Triumph over your status quo. Revel in the possibilities that await you.

Laurie Leinwand, MA, LPC, CC
Ideas 2 Action, LLC
Make it happen!

973-343-6287
laurie@ideas2action-coaching.com
www.ideas2action-coaching.com

Laurie Leinwand founded Ideas 2 Action, LLC and helps women move through transitional phases in their lives triumphantly. She specializes in inspiring and empowering moms to rediscover who they are so they can successfully build their best lives outside of parenting.

Laurie graduated from the University of Pennsylvania with a degree in psychology. To pursue her true passion of helping people move their lives forward, she became a licensed professional counselor and a certified coach. Laurie is a member of the International Coach Federation (ICF) and the American Counseling Association (ACA). Despite running two businesses, Laurie identifies herself as a stay-at-home mom.

Laurie helps clients move from stuck, overwhelmed and confused to focused, motivated and fulfilled. She believes you do not need to settle for mediocrity and that the power to live to your full potential rests in *your* hands. Laurie provides workshops on *Jump Starting Your Life, The Secrets to Saying No* and *Making Friends with Change*. Go to her website to gain access to her free ebook, *7 Spectacular Steps to Getting Unstuck.*

Create Your Rapid Turnaround!

Six Steps to Change Your Life

By Anne Kjellgren

I see so many people today going through life on autopilot. They feel like victims or try to endure life, often by "playing by the rules" or by playing the part they believe they must play. My passion is to show people that their life does not have to be this way and what to do about it.

Global consciousness has increased to a level we have never experienced before. While there are exceptions, the vast majority of us live without worry of acquiring food, water or shelter. We know we can survive, yet we want more. We want to replace that empty feeling with joy and fulfillment. We want a life of purpose and meaning.

Most of us heed the calling for living our divine purpose in one of three ways:

1. Early Knowing. A few of us experience a strong pull right from the start—a knowing of who we are and why we are here.

2. Positive Reinforcement. Some make a conscious choice to live their highest path and purpose in response to a positive event in their lives where they see the opportunity to experience even more joy.

3. The Breaking Point. Most of us tend to ignore all the clues our soul has given us. Extreme pain arrives in our lives when finally we ask, *Isn't there more to life than this?* We are left with the decision of moving from pain and despair to joy and purpose.

You see, the opposite of life is not death. Death is actually a transformation. The opposite of life is being asleep. Not only do I recognize this as a universal truth, I can also tell you this from firsthand experience.

When I was 32 years old, my life took a wild turn. My oldest sister was diagnosed with cancer. One month after she passed, my only remaining sister was diagnosed with an unrelated terminal cancer. I spent five years fighting cancer with them while bringing up three children under the age of five. At the end of it all, I was left with a broken family, legal battles, a business I had inherited that I was not sure I wanted, and my marriage was at the breaking point.

I had lost both my sisters and my two best friends. I felt like I was responsible for so much and receiving support from no one. All my friends and family had gone back to their lives within hours, yet my life would never be the same. I was in shock with the amount of profound loss that I had experienced. In addition to losing my loved ones, I had lost all the time with my children as they grew up. I had also lost the closeness in my marriage and even my history. I no longer had people with whom to share my childhood stories.

My Wake-up Moment

One day I woke up. I woke up in the truest sense of the word. I was lying in bed about three weeks after my middle sister's funeral. I was just not functioning well and then I woke up.

It may sound simple, however I realized one thing that totally turned it all around: *I had a choice.* I could choose who I wanted to surround myself with, I could choose what to do with the business, I could choose whether to be in my marriage or not. I had control over all of it. It did not have to control me!

Although we lived in a very nice home on a lovely little cul-de-sac with friendly neighbors, it was not me. We had bought that house because it was close to my husband's office. The schools were not able to effectively serve my son, therefore I was currently homeschooling him with the help of his former kindergarten teacher.

I knew I needed to put a few unhealthy relationships behind me. It occurred to me that morning that I needed a fresh start—and a new place to live. That afternoon, my husband, a patient and understanding man, heard me out and agreed we would put our house on the market immediately.

As it turns out, I had worked for years to turn businesses and projects around for my clients and employers. Now it was up to me to turn my life around instead of somebody else's company. Thankfully, I discovered that some of those same principles I had learned in the business realm worked for me, too. I lost seventy pounds, sold my house and relocated to the country. I delegated the bulk of labor in my business and embraced my spiritual gifts. I found a new school that addressed my children's needs and did what I had to in order to salvage my marriage.

After three years of what I call cocooning myself, I returned to coaching in a whole new way. Back in 2001, I started a coaching business helping small business owners get out from under their businesses using my skills in finance, process engineering and software development. In 2012, I added the dimension of mindset mastery and understanding universal principles to support my clients in successful lives and thriving businesses.

What I learned for myself, and see with my clients, is that turning your life around does not need to be a long and arduous process. In fact, I find that ripping off the Band-Aid®, feeling the sting and moving on is far more effective. I believe in a *rapid turnaround*. There is no need to wallow where you are or to linger waiting for something or someone to rescue you. *You* are the answer. Yes, *you* have been the problem.

According to the OxfordDictionaries.com Dictionary, the definition for rapid turnaround is as follows:

Rapid /ˈrap•id/ - Happening in a short time or at a great rate.

Turnaround /ˈturn•a•round/ - An abrupt or unexpected change, especially one that results in a more favorable situation. A complete reversal of a situation or set of circumstances.

While it may take years of floundering, seemingly making mis-takes or mis-creating in your life, by changing your view of things, you can radically change your experience. You can transform your life overnight!

> *"Don't feel sorry for yourself if you have*
> *chosen the wrong road, turn around."*
> **—Edgar Cayce, American father of holistic medicine**

Let me introduce Julie, a culinary graduate, who ditched her minimum wage cashier's job so that she could launch her own money-spinning business as a personal chef—all while she cleaned my house. Julie was young and came from a background where stability and insurance benefits were important values. She had the idea that she needed to "work her way up" in the world and pay her dues.

Julie was a young woman who at 22 had been told she had a chronic illness that would leave her on crutches. It would also crush her dream of ever becoming a chef. She did not accept that diagnosis and went through two surgeries, developed her own healthy cooking and hired a personal trainer to help her increase her flexibility and stamina. I met Julie after she had already lost over sixty pounds and was looking for part-time work.

Not long after Julie began preparing homemade, healthy, gourmet meals for my family and helping around the house, I asked her one afternoon why she was not preparing food as her full-time career. She told me that was her dream, however she was still young. She needed to be responsible and have a job with some benefits while she worked her way up. This was Julie's limiting belief.

With some encouragement and support, Julie, now my client, immediately began to sign new clients and identify opportunities that more closely aligned with her vision. Within a few short months, she created the business she dreamed of and a blog inspiring people with her miraculous recovery. Julie became engaged and created real stability and freedom in her life!

How can you create these same results in your life? Here it is, plain and simple.

Six Steps to Creating Your Rapid Turnaround

1. Take Responsibility
The first step is to accept responsibility. It may seem like misfortune has "happened to you." However, universal law dictates that you

attract the exact experience you need at any given time in your life. How does it choose which experiences to present to you? It doesn't. You do.

Your job is to see how—or better yet—simply accept that you created this. You created this situation. You created these relationships. You created this crisis. The good news is you can now create something else.

> *"Watch carefully and see what it is you are really asking for."*
> —*A Course in Miracles,* **a non-secular self-study course**

Rather than looking at your current circumstances as a mistake or a failure, you have the opportunity to see this as a time to grow and prepare for the next phase in your life that will create what you do want.

2. Embrace Choice

For me personally, this is a pivotal concept and I hope you will also see the immense power that God has bestowed in us by being able to choose freely.

Frequently, people tell me that they are not able to create what they say they want in their lives because of a controlling spouse, a dead-end job, an unsupportive family, low bank balance or any number of reasons—excuses, that is.

Let me set you straight right here, right now. You absolutely have complete and all-encompassing power over your life. What you may not like is the idea of the discomfort these decisions could potentially create for you. By making choices for the life you really want, you threaten your security, acceptance or the possibility that someone could withhold their love from you.

> *"The truth is that you are responsible for what you think,*
> *because it is only at this level that you can exercise choice."*
> —*A Course in Miracles,* **a non-secular self-study course**

You may think you are stuck. This is also untrue. You may feel stuck, certainly, however the truth is that you always have choice, in every single moment.

3. Understand the Why in Your Life and Clarify Your Compelling Vision

This is where what I call the juice comes in. You have identified the what in your life—what you want to create for yourself. What will inspire you to create that is the why.

You have taken responsibility for your past choices and for the experiences and situations that this has created for you in your life. To illustrate this concept, we will use a simple metaphor. First, you took responsibility and became fully conscious. You have now awakened from a long nap. You now want to get up and go for a drive. Your choices for the kind of life you want is represented by a new car. However, this still is not yet enough to get you to your destination. The why is the inspiration. The why is your fuel.

A great way to assess this is to ask yourself, "What will it cost me if I don't make this change a part of my life?" (see Laurie Leinwand's chapter, Making Friends with Change on page 73)

4. Assume Success. Have a Strong Belief

According to *A Course in Miracles,* a non-secular self-study course that leads you to find and embrace your own unique spiritual path, published in 1992 by The Foundation for Inner Peace, "Any decision of the mind will affect both behavior and experience. What you want, you expect. Your mind does make your future."

This passage shows us that when we are clear and decisive on what we want and value, we will change our behavior as well as our experience. This is done through raising your vibrational state which draws the necessary people and opportunities into your experience. When you believe without a doubt that you will have something, the universe has no choice except to obey. Your mind does indeed make your future.

5. Stay in the Present: Take One Day, Hour, Minute at a Time
As we embark on our journey, one thing tends to slip us up more than any other: doubt. We doubt ourselves, we have doubts about what has happened in the past and we have doubts about what could happen in the future.

> *"The time is now."*
> **—A Course in Miracles,**
> **a non-secular self-study course**

The best remedy for doubt is to stay in the present. The past cannot be changed and the future has not happened yet. Conserve your energy. Focus. Stay in the present. Your next step will be revealed once it is needed. For now, simply concern yourself with what is at hand and no more.

6. Course Correct All Along the Way
One of the critical errors I see people make all the time is that they want all of the answers before they get started. We want a guarantee. That is human, in many respects. We are hard-wired for safety and security.

Remember, you have not worked out all the details on your GPS— your vision of the outcome. Rather, you have started out on your journey with your beautiful, new car. As you near your destination, there has been an accident and the road you are traveling on has been closed. What do you do now?

According to *A Course in Miracles,* "Lead us not into temptation" means "Recognize your errors and choose to abandon them by following my guidance."

Your GPS tells you this is the best route, yet you are not moving and there is no sign of progress anytime soon. What do you do? Make another Rapid Turnaround! The point I am making here is that if you waited to have all the information before embarking on your journey, you would never leave. In all likelihood, you would still miss something because you can't predict everything. Life happens. I suggest that the best course is to identify your destination, get going and course correct all along the way.

Let's Get Started

Here are six strategies to help you change your life and find your purpose. Taking action on these tips can replace that empty feeling with joy and fulfillment.

1. Write down all those things in your life that are not working or that you would like to change. Write about how you want your life to look. Get into the details. What does your day look like? Take a moment to review. Do you see where you are responsible for each of your choices and your current results?

2. Assess the gap between your current reality and your desire. What do you need to change? What choices will you need to make?

3. Ask yourself why you want to make these changes? What is your life meant to be about?

4. Take time each day—even just a few moments at a time—to visualize yourself at your destination/goal and really feel into it. This raises your vibrational state.

5. Stay in the present. This liberates you. A great way to anchor yourself in the now is to breathe. Breathe in for four counts, hold for four counts and release for eight counts. Repeat twice. Notice how that feels.

6. Congratulate yourself on embracing this opportunity. It is no accident that you found this material now. You are ready to move forward!

To find the meaning in your life and live it with purpose, I encourage you to review the six steps in this chapter. Take responsibility to create something new for yourself, and embrace the choices you make. Discover your why and believe in your own success. Stay in the present and allow yourself to correct your course along the way. Create Your Rapid Turnaround and love your life!

Anne Kjellgren
Your Rapid Turnaround
Intuitive Executive Coach

214-883-8833
anne@yourrapidturnaround.com
www.yourrapidturnaround.com

Anne Kjellgren (*chell*-gren) is a speaker, author, coach and innovator in her business, Your Rapid Turnaround. She has a degree in financial management and started in finance and technology during the pre-Y2K boom. She has experience with Microsoft®, Southwest® Airlines, MarchFirst® and numerous small start-ups. She has been creating rapid turnarounds in businesses since 1995.

Anne helps you to take decisive action toward living the life you desire. She supplies the necessary tools and skills to move forward long after you work with her. Anne first coached small business owners and executives in how to get out from under their businesses. Today, she combines those skills with her intuitive abilities to creatively strategize ways to help her clients get unstuck and ditch that empty feeling to raise their standards, increasing their incomes and overall fulfillment.

In addition to creating her life's work, Anne enjoys nature, creating artisan cheeses, looking after her chickens, cheering on her three children and planning her next trip. Download your free audio recording to walk through the visualization process at www.YourRapidTurnaround.com. For more inspiration from *A Course in Miracles,* like Anne's fan page at www.facebook.com/acoolchange.

Inspire, Desire and Discover

Capitalize on Opportunities Using Your Self Image

By Lauren Carbis, AICI, ICF

*L*ife is an adventure of true limitless possibilities. However, many times we feel stuck, not realizing we are standing in our own way. We are preventing ourselves from our destined fulfillment.

You are never alone on the road to discovering your true purpose of being. The universe consistently provides powerful signs that lead you to your destiny. It is whether or not you choose to pay attention that determines the level of your ease and success. There is no such thing as luck or coincidence. Instead, those moments of serendipity are simply messages sent just for you, like breadcrumbs from the universe.

When you learn to listen to yourself in a deeper state of mind, things formulate and allow you to use the creative genius that is already inside you. *Ask and you will receive.* This may sound cliché, however it is also quite true.

This chapter teaches you how to be intentional with your request to know yourself more fully. This helps you identify those defining moments in your life that will be a springboard into the future you deserve. It also brings to light other elements of your life where with a few tweaks and adjustments, you can really shine!

The Core of a Great Self Image

Our ability to create light within the core of our existence directly relates to how we see ourselves and the value and worth we give to our capabilities. This is our infrastructure. Whether we are conscious of it or not, the quality of this inner space is what allows us to develop our own sense of personal worth. Your fundamental framework includes:

- **Your inner dialogue.** This is what we tell ourselves—good and bad.
- **Your sense of discernment and trust.** This refers to the opportunities you allow into your life and your affinity to the unknown.
- **Your cultivation of spiritual fundamentals.** This is your ability to nurture the mind, heart, body and soul.
- **Your authentic connection with others.** This refers to your interest and acceptance in receiving emotional and physical forms of validation and your ability to affirm and validate the same in others.
- **Your ability to imagine the impossible.** This means giving yourself the freedom to believe anything is possible, and then allowing yourself to be inspired to the point of putting a plan into action to take you there. (see Tobey Allen's chapter, Master the Art of Possibilities on page 63 and Beverly Adamo's chapter, Women and Power on page 191)

When you do not place a high enough value on yourself and the very things that fuel your life, we cannot conjure up alternative methods for creating a lifestyle of purposeful success. Set your sights on sources of life, light and energy. Actively stay aware and push away from negativity and darkness.

Remember, whatever you choose to dwell on is what you attract. If you envy what others have and are focusing on what you lack, you only discover more emptiness and get pulled further into a stagnant life. Others who share your mindset begin to share your energy causing a quicker, downward spiral into an unpleasant space.

On the other hand, when you live authentically by focusing on the qualities and gifts that make you unique, you find yourself in the center of life-giving opportunities. You begin to positively affect other like-minded souls by the energy of your life. This is true fearless living!

> *"What we fear doing most is usually what we most need to do."*
> —**Timothy Ferriss, American author of *The 4-Hour Work Week***

Transitioning Your Focus by Empowering Your Core

Your core is the way your infrastructure is designed. We are intricate beings, created with different levels of insight and enlightenment in tune to not only our lives, but also the lives of others who share our space.

In the chakra system, the infrastructure that houses the core of our being is created with seven rooms. The freedom and fluidity we have to maneuver within these rooms is determined by how in tune we are with our authentic selves.

Each of these seven rooms contains one of the greatest gifts we can experience in life. Once we begin to discover and embrace the meaning and life within each space, our energy enhances and brightens the core of our being. This lightens the way to the next room, where we receive even more clarity than the one before.

Our gift-filled rooms are as follows:
- Room 1: Acceptance
- Room 2: Creativity
- Room 3: Commitment
- Room 4: Compassion
- Room 5: Truth
- Room 6: Intuition
- Room 7: Boundlessness

The goal with discovering these gifts that lie within us is not to live them out fully each day. It is simply to be aware of them within us in order to tap into our gifts and fully utilize them when the universe presents the opportunity.

As we begin to live life more authentically, obstacles can interfere with our ability to utilize our gifts effectively. Each room and each gift has its own darkness. If we allow it to enter, it prevents our light from shining through.

The antitheses to our individual gifts are:
• Room 1: Resentment and Rigidity
• Room 2: Passionate Manipulation and Guilt
• Room 3: Anger and Greed
• Room 4: Fear and Attachment
• Room 5: Denial and Abruptness
• Room 6: Confusion and Depression
• Room 7: Grief

By identifying these areas of darkness, you can better align with what creates your inner light. If you find yourself struggling with feelings of acceptance, look for areas in your life where you may feel a sense of resentment or rigidity. Discovering the source of your darkness is how you can eliminate it. Then, the proper light can disperse those shadows.

Likewise, if someone close to you is experiencing anger or a sense of envious greed, you can help shine light into the life of that person by providing a sense of connection and commitment to his or her unique individuality.

To maintain the integrity of your internal structure, here are a few activities you can do to enhance your ability to shine.

- **Take a break.** Spend time observing nature and find moments of pleasure in life. Whether it is a random stranger playing Frisbee® with a pet, a squirrel digging up acorns or a breeze dancing within the leaves of a tree, take time to acknowledge the life around us. Absorb the energy nature provides. This helps strengthen your physical and emotional health.
- **Take a soak.** Restore emotional balance by allowing negative energy to dissolve away into some sea salts and baking soda. I recommend a pound of each for a twenty-minute soak. For additional renewal, add some aromatherapy oils to the mix and relaxing music. This self-nurturing act helps refuel sensuality.
- **Take a walk.** When you need an extra boost of self-esteem, willpower or intestinal fortitude, a bit of brisk walking or t'ai chi, yoga or Pilates can do the trick. The more you can do outdoors in the sun, the better.
- **Take time for affirmations.** It is time to use your voice and self-talk to affirm who you are as a unique individual. Look for something done well and compliment it. Affirm yourself with statements like, *I am worthy of success and all the opportunities the universe has to offer me. I love and accept who I am right now!* (see Linda Ballesteros' chapter, The Secret to Finding Your Bliss on page 11)

What Your Self Image Reflects to the Outside World

If your light within is considered your infrastructure, then the light you reflect is your image, your signature and your personal brand. A great image allows others to be at ease with you and be receptive to what you have to say. It shows reliability, confidence and professionalism. It says, *I trust myself, so you may feel a sense of trust with me as well.* This exterior reflection you offer the world includes:

- **Your sense of personal style.** This includes your wardrobe, choice of colors and complementary styles, fashions and accessories.

- **Your mannerisms and body language.** This includes your ability to exude confidence, assume an authoritative sense when necessary and take active, not passive roles in room dynamics.
- **Your verbal communication skills.** This is your ability to engage others in affirming and encouraging dialogue, exchange valuable information and know when to graciously move on and engage others in conversation.

For the vibrancy of the universe to unfold before you, your outer image and your inner being must be in sync. Although a building may have stunning curb appeal, it does not attract welcomed companions if the interior is in shambles. Likewise, if the interior is worthy of Decorator's Digest®, yet the exterior appears unkempt, it cannot easily attract other like-minded souls.

Several years back I was a makeup artist in Vancouver, Canada, trying to find my way in the fashion industry. I began to do some online research and felt compelled to look further into becoming an image consultant. It wasn't long before I knew without a doubt that the universe was guiding me toward this industry and showing me that it would complement my profession of helping others to both polish and embrace their self-image. This was incredibly energizing to me!

To add to my educational arsenal on the subject of becoming an image consultant, I purchased a book that ended up in the attic of my parent's house, unread. Years after moving to Toronto, Canada, to jumpstart my fashion career, I came face-to-face with the woman who wrote that book. She was teaching the private Image Consulting course I enrolled myself in to learn more about the business.

As we talked, she was able to pull up an email from her archives I had sent her years ago with questions about the courses she taught.

I almost forgot I felt pulled in this direction so long ago and was amazed at the consistency of the universe in revealing this plan.

I called my parents and gave them a description of where this book was in their attic and they were able to find it and send it back to me, home where it belonged. This book has found a special place in my heart and my home, as it confirms a strong belief of mine: the energy, strength and passion you put out into the universe will give you what you want in return. In other words, the image you project is what you will attract and be surrounded with in return.

Creative Alignment Leads to Fulfillment

How do you ensure you are tapping into the opportunities available to create and reflect your light? First, understand what is standing in your way. Just as your internal rooms have personalized enemies, the way you present yourself to the outside world also has detractors that diminish your level of trust, integrity and overall effectiveness.

For instance, some people get into a frame of mind that puts their true worth and potential at war with how they choose to present themselves to the world. They ask, "Why do I have to dress up if that is not who I really am?"

When a well-polished woman walks into a room with a sense of inspiration and pride because of what she has to offer the world, the audience is drawn to that individual's light and captivated by her message.

A willing audience ready to hear you out is a far better use of your energy than trying to overcome a distracting presentation by having to prove yourself to others before they even hear your message.

Without allowing your authentic self to shine through your presentation to the outside world, you give the impression that you do not fully trust yourself. Therefore, others are free to disregard you as well. Ask yourself, *Is my image serving me or sabotaging me?*

You must recognize obstacles to overcome them. Here are some obstacles you may experience:

- **Competition.** For example, comparing your talents or possessions with others and either feeling worse about yourself or superior to others is a dangerous obstacle that eventually consumes your light.
- **Ego.** This is the false perception that you are somehow more valuable as a human being than those around you. This obstacle not only blocks your light, it also passes negative energy to those who share your space. Value must be given equally across the board to all life, all light and all unique individuals.
- **Facades.** Being disingenuous with yourself and others casts shadows over your gifts and unique abilities.

Getting the obstacles out of the way allows energy and light to flow through you to the world around you. Once you take time to evaluate your forward motion in life and eliminate internal obstacles, it is time to address your presentation—your outward presence in this world.

Let your appearance work *with* your unique individuality and creative gifts, not against them. Be acutely aware of your overall presentation. This includes not only your demeanor and personal style, but also it includes the areas in which you dwell.

Your environment is as important as your personal style in regard to sending the right message out into the world. Therefore, be mindful of both. Your home can either contribute to your energy, making you shine brighter, or it can dim your inner light by causing fatigue, dysfunction and even depression if you do not pay it proper care.

Taking all of your energy sources into account, here are some final action steps to further encourage your internal light to shine at full intensity:

- **Find an Image Coach.** Hiring an experienced image consultant can provide you with education, resources and insight that will forever change the way you see yourself externally. The value they provide is priceless and you put an end to questioning your clothing purchases or feeling insecure about how you look. Your self-esteem blossoms when you know that everything you have in your closet is a perfect complement to your natural grace and style.

  An image coach can educate you on perfect colors for clothing, make-up and hair, as well as suggested hairstyles and jewelry. The image coach will also instruct you on your best skirt length, inseam and style of cut for pants and jeans, as well as assist with what is best to wear on special occasions. Confidence in what you wear and knowledge about your body shape and style are huge steps toward embracing the amazing body you have.

- **Hire a life coach.** Finding a coach who utilizes the same principles in life as you do can allow you to break through challenging situations and allow your true self to find the solutions you need to overcome obstacles that have previously seemed immovable. Not only do life coaches provide guidance, they also provide accountability, encouragement and support which can all lead to great personal enlightenment.

- **Do a wardrobe audit.** Schedule a day on your calendar and if you do not have an image consultant, grab a best friend and begin. Eliminate clutter, items that you have not worn in two years, items that look dated and worn and items that are not flattering. Keep in mind that the only things left in your closet should be within your color pallet, complement your body shape and fit your personal style. Look for quality, not quantity.

- **Reorganize your space.** Do a quick study on Feng Shui and de-clutter your home. That alone can increase your energy and bring renewal into your soul. When your environment is full of positive energy, you beckon the gifts of the universe to unfold around you.

No one can be who you are, and you cannot be anyone else. There-fore, be authentically you and open yourself up to the rewards of the universe.

Lauren Carbis, AICI, ICF
Lifescape Image

647-292-7767
lauren@lifescapeimage.com
www.lifescapeimage.com

Lauren Carbis's career path began in the fashion industry. She has a well-rounded education in makeup artistry, marketing, life coaching and image consulting. Dedicated to living a fearless life, Lauren helps others find their confidence that lets their inner light shine.

Lauren was fortunate to work with Giorgio Armani® and Nars® cosmetics. She worked for one of the top marketing companies in Canada and has collaborated with Fortune 500 companies on the importance of identifying, developing and implementing the true value of a brand.

Lauren's knowledge from both the fashion industry and corporate business, along with her natural gifts, contributed significantly to the brilliant results she brings her clients in her self-image consulting firm, Lifescape Image. Specializing in whole self discovery, Lifescape Image encourages people to break through challenging personal situations by focusing on communication and a solution-based approach in aligning their authenticity with their professional objectives. Lauren expertly guides others to increase their confidence and reach the fulfillment they seek. Her clients learn to effortlessly represent themselves by igniting a genuine connection with others through a healthy self-image that projects passion, integrity and purpose.

Achieving Health and Vitality in Your Life

Five Steps to a Healthier You

By Dr. Yvette M. Nadeau, DC, CCSP

*H*ealth is where it all begins. By being healthy, life is attainable. We usually don't give our bodies much concern until something goes wrong. The problem with this is that sometimes the consequences are too great and cannot be reversed. This way of thinking is not living healthy, it is waiting to be sick.

Being healthy takes some planning. *It is preventing the fire rather than putting it out.*

Some ways to achieve health are very easy while other ways are more challenging. Begin your journey by doing the easy steps first and then working toward the more difficult steps using prayer or meditation. You probably have some healthy habits and they only need to be increased while others need to be avoided completely. Keep working on your health plan until it becomes easier and it will eventually become part of your lifestyle. Health is about lifestyle—not what is only good for today. Remember that being healthy does not happen overnight. Every healthy choice leads you in the right direction.

In order to be healthy, build a better foundation. Do not build a house on a "cracked" foundation. I want to describe certain fundamentals and then ways to achieve long-lasting health and vitality. You can catch your star when you learn how to create good health.

Emotional

First you have to believe that you deserve to be healthy. You are an important ingredient to this world and your mission needs to be completed. Realizing your purpose and staying on track to reach your goals brings fulfillment to your life.

Concentrating on what you do in life instead of what others do or do not do allows you to accomplish your goals and gives you inner peace. Surround yourself with positive thoughts and actions. Do not let other people influence you with gossip or judgment. Clear your thoughts and life from negativity by replacing it with positive thoughts. Your thoughts become your actions.

Understand that you are responsible for your outcome and the choices you make. Resist temptations by believing you can achieve health no matter how hard it might seem at first. Be persistent and stay focused on what you want.

Posture

How we sit and lie down is very important to how our body functions. Many people sit at the computer for six to eight hours every day. Your body was not made to be in one position for long hours. This causes stress on the body, sending signals to your brain. In response, your brain sends neuropathic signals to other surrounding muscles to relieve the stress, which causes compensation. Compensation occurs because your other muscles have fatigued. They are now doing a job they are not equipped to do and therefore can fail, causing injury. By the time you feel the pain, your body already went into compensation and adaptation. The injury is already there. The next question is, how serious is it?

Another thing that leads to bad posture is carrying a heavy back-pack or purse. This leads to an increased kyphotic curvature or "hunchback." We see kids in our office telling us they are carrying all of their books in their backpacks because of the limited time they have to get to class. Carrying this much weight on the back causes undue stress on the entire musculoskeletal system. This is even more dangerous for a developing spine and can lead to scoliosis. Carrying a heavy purse on one side causes your body to pull up on the other side, also leading to scoliosis overtime.

This is why it is very important to receive spinal alignments from a chiropractor. The adjustments help restore misalignments, thus allowing blood and nerve impulses to flow at optimal speed. When the body is shifted in different directions, it puts stress on the muscles, ligaments and tendons and compresses the neurovascular supply.

It is like an automobile being misaligned. The car will shift to one side, therefore causing wear and tear on the tires and suspension system. Replacing the tires would be ridiculous, as you would be treating the effect and not addressing the cause. Taking a muscle relaxer, anti-inflammatory or pain pill is doing the same thing. You only address the symptom and neglect the cause. Spinal alignments address the cause rather than cover up your symptoms.

Your sleeping position can either help or hurt your spine because gravity does most of the work for eight hours. Sleeping on your stomach causes a stress on the lower back because there is not enough support for the natural curvature. It also causes stress on the neck and shoulder area because the neck is either turned to the right or left. This reduces the curvature in your neck, causing it to be straight. This can result in early signs of degeneration and nerve impingement. Sleeping on your side causes an unleveling in the pelvis. Using a pillow in between your legs maintains the pelvis in its proper position.

Preventative measures for better posture:

1. Do computer stretches every 30 minutes.

2. Walk around for ten minutes after every hour of sitting.

3. Wear a backpack that is only ten percent of your body weight.

4. Carry a light purse across your chest or on your back.

5. Sleep on your side with a pillow between your legs.

Chemical

Substances like nicotine, alcohol and medication are very taxing on the body. These substances are not made by the body, therefore they put a lot of stress on the liver to detoxify and on the nervous system to function. The body is capable of healing itself. Just look at what a wound does over time.

When people constantly treat their symptoms with a quick fix, their body becomes dependent on the chemical and the process of healing slows. Their body's natural inhibitors and endorphins become less and less, making them more dependent on the substance. Not only have they increased their intake, now they have taken something else to combat the drug-induced illness they are left with. Medication is beneficial for certain ailments, however it becomes dangerous when a pill has become the answer for everything—especially when it is only treating the symptom.

Think of it like this. We sure do not have a shortage of medication. Then why are more people being affected with diabetes, depression, autoimmune disease, cancer and reflux than ever before? The reason is that we are programmed to think that "they" know what is right for us more than we know what our bodies are telling us. It is written up as medical facts, it is in the media. Therefore, how can it not be true, right? Wrong! All it means is that the pharmaceutical companies have big pockets and are capable of convincing or "brainwashing" us. Listen to your body more and less to the next miracle drug.

This is not only happening with prescription medication. Look at the supplements being dispersed. Retail companies are pumping out more and more supplements. However, they often use either an inexpensive form that the body does not absorb or the supplements are synthetic. The companies often use the same manufacturing plant as other retailers and put their own private label on the bottle. Having multiple companies under one manufacturing plant also increases the problem of cross-contamination in the plant or unregulated temperatures during distribution. This leads to allergies or causes the vitamin to be ineffective.

The Internet has made it too easy for consumers to diagnose and shop for themselves. However, did you know this could make matters worse? Taking a vitamin solely on symptoms can lead to over supplementing an incorrect vitamin or mineral. That nutrient could mask another vital nutrient, making it even more deficient.

Make sure you take what you need by doing the proper tests and taking quality supplements, not synthetic forms. Medical doctors can check certain vitamins and minerals through a blood panel. However, this can lead to taking a pill just for a symptom because the testing procedure is not as sensitive. It is like giving a prescription, except in this case people are fooled into thinking this is healthier because it is a supplement. Avoid store bought, Internet and pharmacy-prescribed supplements.

Nutraceutical supplements are safer and sold to you individually through a health care practitioner who is certified or licensed in nutrition. This individual should be looking at your overall health, not concentrating on the disease or the symptom.

Nutrition

Let's first talk about fat and where it is stored. There are two types of fat, visceral and subcutaneous. Visceral fat is the fat around your organs and in your abdomen. This kind of fat is dangerous and causes heart attacks, strokes, diabetes and hypertension. The subcutaneous fat is the kind you see. It is located under the skin and causes dimpling and cellulite. Yo-Yo dieting only increases the visceral fat, thus increasing your risks. The reason diets fail is because they are set up to be temporary. Diets produce fast results so people will be attracted to them. Fast weight loss means more risk to the body, especially the heart, kidney and liver. Safe weight loss should be one to two pounds per week. Otherwise, most of the weight loss is really water weight coming off and not true fat.

We all know we should eat fruits and vegetables. However, do you know why? Fruits and vegetables contain enzymes to help metabolize your food, phytochemicals such as antioxidants to help fight free radicals and vitamins and minerals to achieve healthy bones, tissues and cells. The recommendation of four to six servings of fruits and vegetables per day is only a guideline. Eating more is better!

Water intake is very important for the body to function and thrive. Water input needs to replenish water output. You lose water by sweating, urinating and defecating. You need it for muscles, tendons, ligaments and cell proliferation. You also need it for blood and fluid transportation. We are not camels, our bodies do not store water. When you deprive your body of the water it needs, it takes away from your muscles, tendons and ligaments in order for your cells to function. This dehydrates your body and causes tears and fissures in your muscles, tendons, ligaments and discs. Dehydration on the largest organ, which is the skin, appears as wrinkles. Kidneys need adequate water because they are the body's filtering system.

Water intake varies from one individual to the next depending on age, gender, activity level and weight. The easiest way to know how much water you need is to take your weight and divide it in half. This is the amount of water in ounces you should consume on average. For example, a 100-pound female should drink fifty ounces of water per day. If she drank one cup of coffee and ran two miles per day, she would need an additional four to five cups of water per day, making her total ten to eleven cups per day. As as you can see, you must replace what you lose.

Counting calories is a way to control what you consume. A daily meal should be composed of protein, fat and carbohydrates. Eating an excess of any of these turns into fat. A woman should consume 1200 to 1500 calories per day and adjust it to her activity level. A man should consume 1800 to 2200 calories per day and adjust it to his activity level.

Depriving yourself of the adequate calories means you are making your body deficient in nutrients and energy. It is like filling your gas tank half full, yet expecting to make a trip that would require a full tank. You will only run on fumes. On the other hand, overfilling your body is dangerous as well and leads to cardiovascular problems and diabetes.

Portion size is another way to control how much you consume. For protein, meat should be the size of your fist. Putting your dinner on a salad plate instead of a dinner plate convinces your brain that you have had enough food. By eating your meals slower, you give your brain the chance to catch up to your stomach and realize you have had enough.

Exercise

Exercise is beneficial for many things in the body. Exercising three to four times per week for one hour raises your metabolism, increases cell and hormone production, reduces lipids and makes you look fantastic. Simply adding exercise makes your body 70 percent healthier. Your body's natural hormones and chemicals makes you feel better and repairs your body faster. Your metabolism works for you instead of against you.

Adding exercise means not feeling like you are gaining weight just by looking at a piece of cake. It even means you will be losing weight while you sleep. Cholesterol levels start to decrease along with glucose levels, reducing your risk of heart attack and diabetes.

An exercise program should include a combination of cardio and weight lifting exercises. The cardio portion improves the strength of your heart and lungs while the weights increase your metabolism and bone strength. Exercise lowers both your visceral fat and subcutaneous fat.

You can get some exercise the easy way when you run your errands by parking your car at the back of the parking lot or at least not close to the entrance. You can also park on the opposite side of the mall and power walk to the other side. Use the stairs instead of the elevator at work if your office is on the second to fourth floor. Work yourself up to anything higher than the fourth floor. Move your television remote control around so you have to get up from time to time. If you want to lose weight the healthy and long-term way, remember to get up and start moving! (see Angeli Fitch's chapter, Persistence Pays on page 169)

12 Healthy Tips for a Healthy You:

1. Eat three small meals and two snacks during the day to raise metabolism.

2. Eat four to six servings of fruits and vegetables per day.

3. Exercise for one hour three to four times per week.

4. Increase your water intake to half your body weight in ounces.

5. Eliminate carbonated drinks.

6. Reduce or eliminate caffeine, as it is a diuretic.

7. Watch your calories and sugar.

8. Reduce the portion sizes of your meat to the size of your fist.

9. Take supplements to enhance your food absorption, not to replace it.

10. Reduce or eliminate harmful chemicals.

11. Watch your posture and visit your chiropractor for spinal check-ups.

12. Think positive and stay focused.

Your body is the only one you get. Taking care of it takes preparation and time—and it is definitely worth it in the long run. The effort you put in will bring many years of happiness to both you and your offspring. At first some of these things may be challenging, however with persistence they become easier. Remember, it is your choice. How you live your life is up to you!

Dr. Yvette M. Nadeau, DC, CCSP
Total Chiropractic & Wellness Center

281-242-4476
dr.nadeau@totalchirocare.com
www.totalchirocare.com

Dr. Nadeau became a chiropractor after her mother was injured and only given the option of multiple medications. Of several jobs Dr. Nadeau worked to support her mother, one was at a chiropractic office. Seeing the amazing results when the body is encouraged to heal itself, Dr. Nadeau chose to pursue her dream of becoming a chiropractor.

Dr. Nadeau graduated from Texas Chiropractic College in 2001 with academic honors. She completed a post graduate program toward a diplomate program in clinical nutrition and is certified in sports chiropractic and acupuncture. Dr. Nadeau established Total Chiropractic & Wellness Center in Sugar Land, Texas in 2003. Her integrative approach uses soft tissue therapies, physical medicine, acupuncture and nutrition with chiropractic care to give her patients excellent results. This helps them achieve their goals and live healthier lives.

A renowned international speaker, Dr. Nadeau presents in the United States and Japan. She is president of the Alumni Association for Texas Chiropractic College and a member of the American Chiropractic and Texas Chiropractic Associations. Call for your free consultation to see if chiropractic care can help you achieve better health and live a pain-free life.

From Fear to Fearless

By Sonia Hassey

*B*elieve in yourself and have faith in your abilities! These are the statements I wish I would have heard growing up. They probably would have saved me from a lot of insecurities and struggles that prevented me from reaching my full potential in my earlier years.

I grew up with two brothers, one sister and my parents. My parents were born in Mexico. They understood the value of hard work and both of them worked equally hard to make ends meet. Our home structure was strict. My mother was a very tidy person, everything had to be clean and polished all the time. She did whatever it took to make sure it stayed that way. Which was, of course, difficult for us kids because all we wanted to do was play.

I don't remember receiving affirmation or praise, much less affection, in our home. I never doubted their love for us, however this is what worked for my parents to keep order in their busy lives with four kids.

As I grew into my teenage years, I could only remember being told about the things that I could not do right, which I internalized and believed about myself. I had absolutely no confidence growing up.

I did not realize how much damage that did to my mindset and it set the stage for many years of heartache. (See Jane Inch's chapter Finding Your Voice on page 43)

I believe our Hispanic culture can reflect this behavior. This is how my grandmother reared my mother, and now I realize that this was learned behavior. My mother did not realize it and did not know any better. This is how she knew best. Nonetheless, the lack of praise or affirmation in childhood can be very destructive to your mindset. I spent many years drowning in the misery of my insecurity. This blocked the real person I was created to be and kept me from knowing my true purpose.

> *"You block your dream when you allow your fear*
> *to grow bigger than your faith."*
> **—Mary Manin Morrissey, American speaker, author**
> **and empowerment specialist**

Growing up, I knew when I would become a mother I would always encourage and praise my children and tell them how much they are loved all the time. I knew that I did not want to repeat that negative pattern. Today, I am raising my daughters with that in mind.

A hairstylist since 1985, I also made a commitment to always encourage and praise my clients. It is the greatest feeling in the world for me to see them encouraged when they leave the salon.

Although I had set these great intentions for other people, I was still not feeling confident in myself. Eventually, I started seeing positive results from my impact on others. That is when I decided to really work on myself.

Having had quite enough of being fearful, I decided to get involved in our church youth group by helping out behind the scenes. After a few months, I was asked to teach a youth leadership class. I felt scared and excited at the same time. I began the class with 15 students. To my surprise, I thoroughly enjoyed every minute of it. Even though I taught the class every Sunday for four years, it took me the whole week each time—and much prayer—to emotionally gear up for the next class. Still, it was well worth it. This experience was a life-changing confidence booster. Plus, the relationships I built with the students were unforgettable.

> *"Face the thing that seems overwhelming and you will be surprised how your fear will melt away."*
> **—Dale Carnegie, American writer, public speaker and self-improvement expert**

As the youth group leadership class came to an end, I began to feel sad and discouraged. I did not know what was next for me—but I was about to find out! Right before the class ended, we went to a youth conference. There were many speakers, and one in particular got my attention, Doug Tawlks. He had all the students' undivided attention. When he finished speaking, I gathered up the courage to walk up to compliment him on his speaking and his confidence. After a good conversation with him, he invited me to join him and his wife, Shari, on a trip to the Philippines. He told me he would mentor me for the duration of our stay. This was exciting!

When I told my husband, he encouraged me to go if I really wanted to. Three weeks later, we boarded a plane to the Philippines! I then realized that I took action against all the fears that would have held me back from trying something new. I had no idea what I would experience in the Philippines with my new-found friends. All I knew was that I was ready for change in my life. I just did not know what that looked like yet.

"We can complain because rose bushes have thorns,
or rejoice because thorn bushes have roses."
—**Abraham Lincoln, 16th President of the United States**

The trip was an incredible experience and I met wonderful people. Doug and Shari were wonderful mentors. They helped me recognize the limiting beliefs about myself and proved that I can conquer them. I was asked to speak to a youth group at a church there. This terrified me and I did not want to do it. Being far away from home was a big enough stretch for me. However, Doug convinced me to speak, and I am glad I did. Once again, my action broke that ugly fear that loved to creep up on me.

When you take risks and step outside your comfort zone, you open yourself up to amazing possibilities. I will never forget the enormous impact the experience the Philippines had on my life. It truly catapulted my mindset for the better and I returned home with a whole new perspective. It was the greatest feeling ever.

When I returned to work, I wanted to inspire as many people as I could because I was truly inspired. I wanted to give back what was given to me.

I had a strong desire to learn more about personal development and began to read many books—Dale Carnegie, Dani Johnson, John C. Maxwell, Napoleon Hill, Vincent Norman Peale, the Bible and many others. I felt a deeper hunger to grow and learn more. I also started attending as many seminars as I could. This was a whole new world for me, a world I never knew before and one that I never wanted to leave.

I deeply wanted to change my old ways of thinking and had to go search for ways to do so. In my quest, I have met many wonderful people along the way.

"If you are not in the process of becoming
the person you want to be,
you are automatically engaged in becoming
the person you don't want to be."
—Dale Carnegie, American writer, public speaker
and self-improvement expert

I also took the Dale Carnegie course on human relations. This course broke my fear of public speaking. It catapulted me to a whole new level in my life, taught me a new skill and gave me a new challenge.

I joined a business networking group in my town, which helped me stay connected with people who wanted to grow their businesses. This also kept challenging my public speaking skills.

I memorized scriptures about renewing my mind. I was on a mission to finally live a rich, fulfilling life in mind, body and spirit. I have become so intentional about this that in addition to myself, I also speak positive words to everyone I come across.

I began declaring that every day is going to be an amazing day! I decided to help people think more positively. I help many clients get unstuck from their undesirable situations. Then I guide them to think more positively about their outcome. My favorite breakthroughs are when I help clients discover what they are truly passionate about and encourage them to go and fulfill their dream— and then they do! (see Shontaye Hawkins' chapter, Birthing Your Dreams on page 1)

"A person can succeed at almost anything
for which they have unlimited enthusiasm."
—Charles M. Schwab, American steel magnate

Seeing these results lead me to discover my passion—helping people see their potential and break through their limiting beliefs. This discovery is why I decided to become a certified life coach—the best decision I ever made. I never thought in a million years that I would serve others through my pain. I am now set free from my past and the limiting beliefs that tormented me for years.

I am on a mission to empower women who have fears like I had. My goal is to inspire them to live the abundant life they were meant to live. There is truly something fearless inside me that I never had before. It is the greatest feeling in the world. I am free to be me without fear. I feel I can now conquer anything and I no longer let others' negativity influence me. Now that is a breakthrough all by itself.

Sharing the joy, encouraging others and following my passion manifested into the Women Inspired Network (WIN), a women's network I founded in 2012. There was already a men's club in my town. I decided it would be great to bring women together for the sake of building friendships, adding value to one another through inspiration and cooperation and bringing our resources together to give back to the community.

> *"Take a chance! All life is a chance.*
> *The man who goes the farthest is generally the one who is willing to do and dare. The 'sure thing' boat never gets far from the shore."*
> **—Dale Carnegie, American writer, public speaker and self-improvement expert**

WIN has proven to be a great success from the beginning. The wonderful women on our leadership team use their talents and enthusiasm to make things happen for the community. We welcome all women, as I believe everyone has value and gifts to share with each other and the community.

The most exciting part of WIN is how we challenge ourselves to accomplish our goals. I am proud of our network and so grateful to lead these amazing women.

I am committed to giving back what I have always wanted for myself—encouragement, love and inspiration. Anything is possible when people come together in harmony.

In addition to WIN, a friend and I are manifesting a project, Inspired Futures, to help young adults find their strengths and purpose. We provide them with a blue print for their careers. My heart is full of gratitude.

> *"You were put on this earth to achieve your greatest self,*
> *to live out your purpose, and to do it fearlessly."*
> **—Steve Maraboli, American behavioral scientist,**
> **coach and motivational speaker**

It is my daily intention to stay positive and to never again live a life of fear. The prison walls of my mind have been broken completely. I now see others with a whole new outlook. I see the best in them, because this is how I see myself. I know the importance of living a happy, fun-loving life and to learn to love and consider the best in people.

We were created to have healthy relationships and a healthy soul—our mind, our will and our emotions. The Bible tells us as our soul prospers, our life will prosper. I am living proof of that.

I will never take a single day for granted. Life is too precious. I truly live the abundant life! My passion and purpose is to inspire others to live the abundant life they were meant to live. I am ready to take chances. I will dream big, think big, pray big, believe big! We will see where it all takes me. All I know is that I am ready!

Nine Strategies to Go from Fear to Fearless

My journey from fear to fearless taught me these strategies I can share with you:

1. Take action on your fears.

2. Develop an awareness of your thinking pattern.

3. Speak positive words about yourself every day.

4. Combat your negative mindset with positive thoughts.

5. Be around people who are positive and enjoy life.

6. Pray and memorize scriptures about renewing your mind.

7. Read books on personal development.

8. Be persistent and determined to change.

9. Have faith and courage to step out and reach your enormous potential.

Become fearless and *catch your star!*

Sonia Hassey
Women Inspired Network

soniahassey@gmail.com
www.inspiredfuturescoach.com

Sonia Hassey is a certified life coach, speaker and has a Certificate of Achievement from Dale Carnegie Training in effective communications and human relations. One of Sonia's greatest passions is helping women break free from any fears or limiting beliefs that would hinder them from reaching their full potential and living a rich, fulfilling life.

Sonia is the president of Women Inspired Network. This organization brings women together to build relationships, inspire and network. It is an environment in which women are encouraged to be in service to one another and the community. Sonia is very proud of the great team created by this successful network which has become a strong force for the community.

After teaching youth leadership in her church for four years, Sonia realized her passion for this age group as well. In addition, she founded Inspired Futures, which provides a program for youth and young adults to help them realize their strengths and purpose. It also gives them clarity and helps them remove any obstacles that get in the way of achieving their enormous potential. Sonia has partnered with Anita Radosevich to complete this excellent program.

Tragedy to Thriving

By Tammy Rose Phye

*I*f you are reading this book, chances are you want to thrive in your life. I believe we all deserve to thrive and live our best life and that it is up to us to make that happen.

About twenty years ago, I was engaged to my best friend, lover, and the one person who showed me the true meaning of unconditional love. We were anticipating buying our first house and excited by the prospects of starting a family. My life was unfolding like a Walt Disney fairy tale. I was thriving with a bright future.

At the time, we both worked in the logging industry, he on the tugboats and I as a camp cook. My life changed forever over a single word, "Mayday." There was a boating accident and on that day, Gordy, our dreams, our plans and our life together, drowned.

> *"To change is to think greater than how we feel."*
> **—Dr. Joe Despenza, American neuroscientist,**
> **chiropractor, lecturer and author**

I was lost, alone and trying to recreate my life. The tension was coiled in my jaw, back, hips and legs. My body was holding this mountain of trauma-energy from the tragedy. I knew I had to do something. I had to embrace a process that would move the physical, mental and emotional pain energy out of my body so that I could heal. The process began with self-examination and questions. Now what? What do I want to do? What did my heart want? What good things can come out of this? What am I to learn? How do I gain a new direction? Where is the good in all of this?

The process began by creating a self-care success strategy plan consisting of breathing exercises, meditation, journaling and essential oils. It was a pilgrimage to my inner world where I allowed myself to be filled with light and peace, and to listen to the inner whispers. As my body felt nurtured, safe and cared for, it began to relax and release the pain and tension that had built up following the tragedy.

We experience loss in so many areas of our lives. It could be your career, your business, your finances, your health, your marriage, your pet, your transition to an empty nest or a death of a loved one. Grief and loss impact life on a variety of levels, and we all deal with them somewhat differently.

My loss hit me deep in the heart. I was fortunate. My life with Gordy was completely open and honest and it left no room for regrets, resentments or unfinished business. We lived our time together fully and we appreciated life. This awareness created an unobstructed path for the healing process.

One paramount truth that was revealed during the process was that I had a choice in how I could respond to this life-changing event. I believe all things happen for a reason. Even though this experience did not make sense, nor did I understand why it happened, I granted myself permission to accept Gordy's death. By acknowledging that there was a bigger reason beyond what I could comprehend, I could move forward. If I had remained determined to understand why this happened, I can only imagine the deep and dark depression those thoughts would have created in me.

> *"We must be willing to get rid of the life we've planned*
> *so as to have the life that is waiting for us."*
> **—Joseph Campbell, American mythologist, writer and lecturer**

No one asks for the journey of grief and loss and it is usually unexpected. How you deal with it is what matters. Rather than deny it, look at it and feel the feelings and allow them to flow like a river. Feelings are connected to emotions, always coming and going, it is more the attention and the meaning that we attach to them that determines the outcome.

One technique to help you focus the right attention on your thoughts is to create a mantra. I used, "How can something good come out of this tragedy? May he somehow make a bigger difference as a result of this tragedy, even though I have no idea how that will present itself."

Success Strategies for Dealing with Change

- **Breathing.** Amazingly, when our bodies are in the fight or flight mode, our breathing becomes shallow and we are unable to relax. Begin by taking deep breaths into your abdomen allowing your lungs to expand fully. Focus on being aware of your breath going in and out. Notice the rhythm of your inhale and your exhale to see if there is a difference. The inhale and exhale should be evenly paced. If they are not, examine why that is and concentrate on making them even.
- **Affirmation.** Incorporating an affirmation can be helpful. On the inhale, "I am open to light," on the exhale, "My heart-light shines." If you are not ready for an affirmation, then place a drop of essential

oil on the palm of one hand, rub both hands together and inhale the scent as you breathe. This allows your lungs and brain to be filled with the scent and experience the many qualities and healing attributes of the oil. (see Linda Ballesteros' chapter, The Secret to Finding Your Bliss on page 11)

- **Meditation.** There are so many styles of meditation. The breathing exercise above can also be classed as a type of meditation. All meditation has the ultimate goal of creating a place of calm, clearing the mind and quieting the mental chatter to promote awareness and relaxation. (see Angeli Fitch's chapter, Persistence Pays on page 169)

"In today's world, sometimes you can't flight, you can't flee.
The only way out is to learn to flow."
—Dr. Robert Eliot, American author, cardiologist
and co-founder of the Institute of Stress Medicine

- **Essential Oils.** They are the life blood of a plant. The most common method of extraction is distillation of the plant material. This creates a highly concentrated oil that is added to a carrier oil when used directly on the skin. Essential oils have the ability to calm, sedate, stimulate and regenerate.

"Scent...is not only biologically the oldest but also the
most evocative of all our senses. It goes deeper than conscious
thought or organized memory and has a will of its own which human
imagination is compelled to obey."
—Lauren Van Der Post, Afrikaner anthropologist,
farmer, war hero and political adviser

When scent enters the nose, it travels through three stages within a split second. The odor molecules bind to the olfactory epithelium, consisting of more than 10 million nerve endings. These respond to the aromatic molecules. The nerve impulses are then sent to the olfactory bulb at the base of the brain, to the cerebral cortex, and to the limbic system—the seat of emotions and memory. The limbic system is home to the amygdala and the hypothalamus. The amygdala is where our instinctual behavior, emotions, and memories lie. The hypothalamus controls the autonomic nervous system, body temperature, appetite and thirst. The hypothalamus sends chemical messengers into the blood, releasing hormones that regulate body functions. Connecting the relaxing, rejuvenating and calming scents to our healing journey profoundly links us to that oldest sense.

There is another aspect known as subtle aromatherapy, which utilizes the energetic nature of the plant. This is a form of vibrational medicine. The energetic quality is not just based on the chemical constituents in isolation. It examines the energetics of the plant. People have used aromatic qualities of plants in religious rituals for thousands of years in an attempt to promote feelings of oneness with the universe and God. More than one hundred different essential oils are available today. Thankfully, your collection need not be that plentiful to have a powerful impact. Pick your oils based on their therapeutic use, how you plan to use them, or what most appeals to your senses. You may want to try an interesting experiment. Choose an essential oil that you do not care for to see how it connects to you and your situation.

Here, I share my favorite essential oils for dealing with grief, loss, change and transition. I invite you to find some essential oils that speak to you and begin your exploration.

- **Lavender (angustifolia)** Lavender is good for healing scratches and burns. This nurturing essential oil warms the heart and helps to soothe the emotions.
- **Cedar (cedrus atlantica)** Cedar promotes calm, a sense of grounding, and protection. Cedar also gives a feeling of courage and strength. Cedar is a comforting oil.

- **Frankincense (boswellia carterii)** This oil gives a sense of protection, cleanses one's aura or a room, and helps to slow the breath. When you slow your breathing, you are encouraging a connection to the unconscious during meditation.
- **Geranium (pelargonium graveolens)** This brings balance and harmony to the emotions. It is also connected to hormonal activity; thus creating a sense of calm.
- **Vetiver (vetiveria zizanioides)** Vetiver is calming, grounding, and provides protection. It helps when you feel threatened by change. It will aid in sustaining and re-establishing balance between your heart, body and mind.
- **Cypress (cupressus sempervirens)** It provides support for change bringing strength and comfort during a transition. When the past and future seem diametrically opposed in the present, Cypress provides support.
- **Lemon (citrus limonum)** Lemon helps to clear confusion, bring clarity and invigorate. It is good for cleansing a room.
- **Orange (citrus sinensis)** Orange promotes lightheartedness and a sense of joy. If you want to move stagnant energy, then Orange is an excellent choice.
- **German chamomile (matricaria recutita)** This oil gives freedom by helping you to let go and relax. This is a blue essential oil that connects with the throat—it is no wonder that it can support calm when speaking the truth.
- **Peppermint (mentha piperita)** Peppermint is stimulating to the mind and inspires purpose. It aids in digesting both food and ideas. Its cooling sensation helps bring clarity to muddy confused thoughts or feelings.
- **Spikenard (nardostachys jatamansi)** Use this oil when you are seeking help in overcoming all types of grief or trauma. It promotes hope and resilience by helping to rebuild the foundation and settle the heart.

Using Essential Oils

Place a drop of your preferred essential oil on your hands and rub them together. Cupping your hands around your nose and mouth, breathe deep, relaxing breaths. Take a mental inventory of any changes you experience. Notice where the scent travels and how it makes you feel. Take a few minutes to breathe with your hands down by your sides, and then re-introduce the scent by bringing your hands again to your face. If you find your thoughts scattered and distracted throughout your deep breathing session, focus on this mantra: as you inhale, think, *I allow light in* and as you exhale, *my light flows.* This steadies your thoughts.

Incorporating a journaling practice at this time helps to enhance and develop your essential oil experience. What did you notice? Did your breathing steady? Did your agitation subside? Did it increase? Focus on what you want in your life. From a state of calm and relaxation, you can solve your greatest challenges. In this state of deep stillness, you can determine what you need to do to become more resilient, more comforted and more aligned with how you can live your best life.

I recommend this aromatic spa treatment for your body and brain any time, and it especially helps when you are on an emotional roller coaster. Vetiver or Spikenard are fantastic if you are agitated and are having difficulty settling your physical, mental or emotional energy. When dealing with grief and loss, place a drop of Spikenard on the top of your head, the crown, the forehead, over your heart, and on the bottom of your feet. An inner calm begins to appear. Trust your nose. If a scent creates more anxiety or agitation, discontinue its use for a time.

*"The greatest weapon against stress is our ability
to choose one thought over another."*
—**William James, American philosopher
and psychologist**

Silver Linings

I did not like what happened to me and would not wish it on anyone. However, I was on the path to healing and wellness. The light was starting to shine again and I was willing to look for the silver lining. Creating a self-care success strategy is important and not just when we are faced with sudden life changes. An ongoing strategy benefits our fast-paced daily living. It can slow the aging process, decrease stress, help us feel more fulfilled and fill our lives with vitality. It also cultivates an openness to positive and healing thoughts, which is ideal for identifying the silver linings in every situation.

Lessons Learned

1. Life is always changing. Our feelings of darkness will pass. When nothing makes sense, hold on to the knowledge deep within you that a bigger purpose is at work. When you become curious and less judgmental, your reality changes and becomes more flexible. You begin to see patterns and connections between yourself, life and nature. You may also find your values changing.

2. We are resilient beings. According to the article, *The Art of Resilience* in *Psychology Today,* May 1, 2003, "Resilient people do not let adversity define them. They find resilience by moving towards a goal beyond themselves, transcending pain and grief by perceiving bad times as a temporary state of affairs." As my mother used to say, "We are never given more then we can handle." Adversity helps us build character.

3. A life lived with gratitude is a full life. From my time with Gordy, I now know what it means to share unconditional love, compassion and understanding. I want the best for those around me and I have been graced with countless blessings. My loss and grief have led me to a career that I love. I have more compassion and a deeper understanding of the struggles my clients face simply because I have experienced a similar path.

4. Take some time to create your success strategy. Plan and implement some of the ideas I have shared with you along with those that you have already learned from other authors in this book. Allow your resilience to grow—even more—to thrive; let your star shine brightly.

> *"The only way to predict the future is to create it."*
> **—Dr. Joe Dispenza, American neuroscientist**

Be willing to learn, forgive, let go and love again regardless of the obstacles you have faced. I am thankful that our paths have crossed and if you would like to share your defining moments, insights, or story with me, I would love to hear from you.

Tammy Rose Phye
Lifestyle Harmony

250-754-3930
tammy@lifestyleharmony.ca
www.lifestyleharmony.ca
tragedytothriving.com/casgift

A dynamic inspirational speaker, workshop leader, and founder of Lifestyle Harmony, Tammy Rose Phye empowers people to take action to live their dreams and their best life. From corporate burnout to the death of her fiancé, Tammy speaks from the heart and can connect in a deep and profound way to her audience and clients. She shares the techniques, tools, and strategies that helped her overcome great loss and stress to help others live their lives with greater peace, resilience, and passion.

As a transformational change agent, Lifestyle Wellness expert, essential oil therapist, massage therapist, certified Pranic Healer and a gifted intuitive healer, Tammy cultivates an environment of self-growth and empowerment. She has assisted countless busy entrepreneurs and professionals to experience a more calm and energized life.

Tammy's unique combination of professional training, life experience and passion provide a strong foundation from which to help clients move to new levels of self-awareness, passion, personal growth and inner peace. Tammy takes living her best life to heart and in her spare time you can find her touring on her motorcycle or traveling to exotic locations like Bali. Tammy has a free gift for you at tragedytothriving.com/casgift.

Creating Powerful Goals to Catch Your Star

How to Turn Your Visions into Reality

By Erin Summ, CPC

*D*id you know your brain *thrives on* goals? It constantly searches for the next thing to help you stretch and move forward in life. Goals keep you focused, moving forward and striving to reach your dreams. Without something solid to focus on, you spend your time off track from your goals, feeling like a Stretch Armstrong® doll, being pulled in random directions, with no place to go. Setting goals is key to building confidence—a first step to success.

> *"The top ten percent of successful people think about what they want and how to get it, most of the time."*
> —**Brian Tracy, American motivational speaker and author**

Successful people, whether they be in life or business, think in terms of action—*What steps do I need to take to create what I want? How do I turn this dream into reality? What is next?* They take deliberate action by making plans and consistently creating new goals to move forward. Less than three percent of Americans have written goals and less than one percent review them daily. The highest achieving people in the world have written goals and review them every day.

What is a Goal, Anyway?

What exactly is a goal? A goal is not *I would like a brand new, shiny black car*. That is just wishful thinking. A goal is *I will own a 2014, BMW M6 convertible in metallic black by March 15, at 5 p.m.* See the difference? A goal is filled with details, it is specific, measurable and time-oriented. When a goal is not well-defined, your brain does not know what to focus on or create. Therefore, it stands still.

Six Steps to Creating Powerful Goals

Step One: Make a Decision
When setting goals, it is imperative to make a clear, solid decision about what you want to achieve. When you make a decision, your brain immediately gets to work to see it through to fruition. It seeks tools to help you, ideal people to support you, and gets your creative juices flowing.

Step Two: Write it Down.
When you commit your goals to paper, it solidifies them in your mind. It keeps you working toward their completion and helps you keep track of your progress. (see Laurie Leinwand's chapter, Making Friends with Change on page 73)

Super Tip: Write your goals and post them in multiple places where you will see them every day. Sticky notes are great! Use brightly colored notes which cause you to notice them, creating a constant focus on the outcome. Post them on your bathroom mirror, kitchen cabinets, in your car, at your desk and anywhere else you will see them multiple times per day.

Important: Make sure to read your goals out loud at least three times every day to stay laser focused on the outcome.

Step Three: Create a B.A.M! S.M.A.R.T Goal
B.A.M! S.M.A.R.T is an acronym for the criteria to use anytime you create a goal. This ensures you step out of your comfort zone, sets you up for success and ensures you stay on track while reaching big enough.

B: Bull's eye. This is your ultimate, target goal. It stretches you to a place of growth, which is vital for your success.

A: Acceptable. This is the minimum you will accept as an outcome. You must decide what is acceptable when you initially write your goal. Sometimes it can take a few tries to reach your bull's eye, which is perfectly fine. When stretching beyond your comfort zone, this is normal because you are in new territory. Your learning curve is steeper than with something you are already comfortable with.

M: Midway. This is the halfway point between acceptable and bull's eye.

S: Specific. When you create a goal, make it as specific as possible, as in the example about acquiring the BMW. It is so clear, you can literally picture what that car might look like.

M: Measurable. The goal must be measurable in order to track where you are in the process. Some examples are pounds lost, money in the bank, a particular task completed, or money saved toward a vacation or car. For instance, *I will have $10,000 in my savings account by December 15 at 2 p.m.*

A: Attainable. Make sure your goal is large enough to expand your capabilities, yet reachable based on your current circumstances to ensure attainability.

R: Reasonable. Ask yourself, *Is it reasonable for me to reach this goal within the time frame I am setting it for? Do I have the time, resources and support to accomplish this goal the way I am setting it up?*

T: Time-Oriented. Set a specific date and time for the completion of your goal.

Super Tip: Remove "fail" from your vocabulary. If at any point you do not fulfill any part of your goal, it is okay. You gave it your best shot, learned and grew from it and that has great value. I encourage you to look at what you learned and how you can apply that to improve next time. Also, you can modify your goal at any time if you are not on track in any area.

Step Four: Make it Believable

When creating a goal, make sure you believe it is achievable for you at the time. If it is too big, you may become overwhelmed and give up before you begin. Make it something that broadens your comfort zone, helps you grow as a person, feels like something you can accomplish and excites you to work toward. Set yourself up for success by keeping it believable for you. As you stretch and grow, your goals get bigger and remain believable.

Step Five: Break it Down

How do you eat an elephant? One small bite at a time. When creating a large goal, you will want to break it down into small chunks to avoid overwhelm and burnout. When you look at the whole goal, it might seem daunting, however when you break it down into smaller bites, it seems more doable. This helps you to keep moving on it. I cover this step in more depth in the section on breakthrough goals.

Step Six: Ask Yourself How

Creating a goal can be exciting and sometimes daunting because it might be something that you have not done before. You might have doubts pop up and you could find yourself wondering *How am I going to accomplish this?* That is actually the *best* question to ask!

When you ask yourself questions about how you will complete your goal, your brain actually gets creative and searches for answers for you. Before you know it, ideas flow to you. I suggest carrying a small notepad with you so that when you think of ideas, you can write them down. You can also download a voice recording app on your phone to talk through your ideas when you are on the go. I recommend writing everything down when you can, in case technology fails, to avoid losing your precious ideas.

Creating a Breakthrough Goal

There are many types and sizes of goals. They can be long-term, short-term, big, small, life, business and breakthrough. A breakthrough goal is something that will cause a quantum leap for your life, your business or both. It is a goal that is crazy big, probably scary and exciting all at the same time.

Here is an example of how to create and breakdown a business breakthrough goal using BAM! SMART.

Let's say you are an entrepreneur with a start-up business in its second year. The first year, the business brought in $25,000 in revenue. For the second year, your goal is to have $100,000 in revenue by December 31 at 11 p.m.

Bullseye is $100,000
Acceptable is $50,000
Midway is $75,000

Specific: Your goal is specific because it states an exact number you want to reach—$100,000—as well as the date and time by which you will reach it—December 31 at 11 p.m.

Measurable: It is measurable because you can track dollars you bring in within the timeframe set.

Attainable: It is attainable because you have built a lot of momentum in the first year and you have created programs to easily bring people in the door. You are implementing ideas to create more revenue and have hired an assistant so you can concentrate on more money-making activities. You have created a buzz within your ideal community of clients and new business is flowing in.

Reasonable: You feel your goal is reasonable because you have so much momentum built, are implementing programs and have many speeches on the calendar to build your business.

Time-Oriented: You have until December 31 at 11 p.m. to reach your goal.

The next step would be to divide the number of dollars you plan to bring in by the amount of time you have, in this case, 12 months. Break down the revenue you need for each month and come up with a monthly plan for how you will create the revenue, for example the number of new clients, speaking gigs or revenue from programs and products. Create a spreadsheet to track income, create plans and use a large, one-year calendar to see your schedule for your year with one glance.

Your Mindset: What are You Focusing On?

When you are working toward completing a goal, make sure you have a positive mindset and are concentrating on all the good coming to you. This is a great way to do anything in life because focusing on the good attracts more of the same. Here are four tips to help you:

Tip 1: Focus on the Goal
Have you ever heard the phrase, "Like energy attracts like energy?" This means that whatever you focus on will be attracted into your life.

When you are working toward a goal, sometimes things go smoothly. This is exciting and fires you up! Other times, however, things go the opposite of how you wanted them to and this can be disappointing. What is important is understanding ahead of time that there will be ups and downs. When things do not quite go how you want, to shake it off, know it is part of the process and focus on all the things that have and are going well. Focusing on the roadblocks destroys your motivation and makes your goal feel impossible. You may even feel like giving up. It is imperative to see the roadblocks as necessary for you to learn, grow and discover what will and will not work, and to move on. Concentrate on all the good things coming your way. Appreciate what is working and the excitements, no matter how big or small.

What are you focusing on?

Tip 2: Overshoot the Goal
Most people tend to decide on a goal, plan to hit that bull's eye, and stop there. I encourage you to shoot through it, not merely go to it. This ensures that you hit the goal and then take it further and into your next goal.

Tip 3: Expect Success

When you have a goal, expect to be wildly successful. Again, like energy attracts like energy. Expect victory, work toward it and it will come. Expecting success makes you more creative, energized and hopeful than worrying about not achieving your goal.

Tip 4: Have a *Why* and a Vision

Your *why* and your vision are the most powerful pieces of your goal. Your reason for wanting to accomplish your goal is your *why*. It must be highly compelling to keep you on track. I suggest including loved ones in your *why* because it increases your drive. Sometimes just doing something for ourselves is not strong enough to keep us moving forward.

Your vision should also include your *why*. Your vision could be about life, business or what life would look like when you reach your ultimate goals. What are you working toward? What is your ultimate vision for your life? Include as many of the senses as you can in your vision. What do you see, smell, taste, feel and hear? The more detailed you are, the stronger the vision. An example could be, *I am at my vacation beach house. I am sitting in my blue lounge chair on the beach, first thing in the morning. It's still a bit chilly, but the sun warms my body. I stick my toes in the sand, take a sip of hot coffee and breathe in the fresh ocean air. I hear the waves crash upon the shore, and think about how grateful I am to have a thriving business that allows me to have such a wonderful life.* The vision can literally be seen and felt in the body. The more clear your vision, the better.

Every day, concentrate on your vision for at least one minute at a time—in the morning before getting out of bed and at night before going to sleep. Your brain does not know the difference between actually doing something and only visualizing it and this actually makes the brain achieve more.

Now that I have given you a few tools for getting clear with your vision and creating solid goals, I encourage you to spend some time mapping out your plans for both your short-term and long-term goals. Brainstorm and map them out on paper and commit to working toward their completion every day. If you follow the steps I have laid out for you in this chapter, your new-found confidence will amaze you and you will easily move toward meeting your goals and fulfilling your vision.

Erin Summ, CPC
Success Coach, Speaker, Author
Business training and confidence
breakthroughs for women life coaches

erin@erinsumm.com
www.erinsumm.com

Erin is passionate about making a difference in the world. She helps women life coaches in their first year of business who are challenged with getting clients because they lack confidence as a new coach, yet have a calling to change the world. Everything Erin does is about confidence breakthroughs so that women can start seeing results, getting clients, and fulfilling their vision.

Erin believes that in order to truly thrive in life and business, one must first develop a strong foundation of deep roots. To her, this means one must have confidence, positive beliefs and mindset, be adaptable and resilient, and have a solid network of outside support. Erin says, "the deeper the roots, the sweeter the fruits."

Erin gives dynamic, educational and empowering presentations and workshops on Confidence Breakthroughs, Mindset Mastery, goal setting and destroying blocks to turn one's vision into reality. She holds a bachelor's degree in psychology and is a Certified Professional Coach through the Institute for Professional Excellence in Coaching.

Master the Art of Taking Action

By Michelle Barr

*W*hen you want something better, something more for yourself, the most important first step is to realize that it is up to you to create it. Then know you can do that starting right now. In working with my private coaching clients, I find that positive changes and new results can begin to show up within the first thirty days. By the end of ninety days of working consciously to create a better life, their lives are more satisfying, fulfilling and joyful.

No matter what you want to do, no matter what you want to work on, no matter what area of your life in which you are ready to make changes, the principles and processes to do so are the same.

There is good reason why people who teach success principles tell you to take action. It is the place where dreams become reality, where desires are made manifest. Taking action is the only way to bring your vision into your waking world.

Action is what manifests things for you on the third-dimensional plane, right here, to show up in your life. However, you do not want to take just any action. You do not want to just be doing, doing, doing. Instead, learn to receive inspiration and experience the power that comes with taking Inspired Action.

It is important to first develop your gifts, abilities and skills. Then, learn to use the IOA formula—Intention, Opportunity, Action. The IOA integrates these three action steps with the use of your intuition, your energy and your mindset. The result is magic!

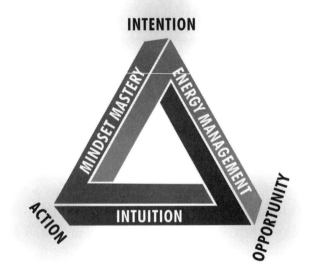

This allows you to live into your dreams and vision here and now. You let them show up in your physical world. You learn first to reconnect your spiritual and creative energy with your physical reality. Then you learn how to master the art of taking action. Remember, not just any action—*inspired action.*

You may wonder if this formula is right for you or if it can help you right now. Perhaps you doubt you are ready or that all your ducks are in a row. You may have made space for this in your life plan for later. Stop thinking like this because I am happy to tell you that this strategy works whether you are a baby-stepper or a ledge-leaper. The results are the same because it all works with your energy.

You must get to the *action*. It takes third-dimensional action to create third-dimensional results. It takes massive third-dimensional action to create massive third-dimensional results. That means you have to come out of your head and come out of the ether and make things happen for you in real time. It is so much better that way. Really.

Get Unstuck From Your "Stuff"

My passion is to get people out into the world using their gifts. You can really become stuck when you put yourself out there and ask for something in return. This is when all your programs, beliefs, patterns and habits related to your value and your worth start showing themselves. You are stuck, having a personal or spiritual crisis or getting in your own way. However, you also have a vision, you know you have been called to do something and you are trying to step out and do it.

That is when mastering the art of taking action really works. That is when you can get in touch with your why, connect in with your vision, your mission, your dreams and your own personal truth, and act from a place of purpose.

The minute you hear that calling and respond, as soon as you step out and step up, when you have big dreams and big visions, you set big goals and intentions, everything inside you that is not in alignment with that comes up. I call it "your stuff," and it is part of the process.

This part of the process can feel negative. It can come with thoughts like, *I'm not strong enough to do this now* or *I'm trying to do this and look what's getting in the way.* You might think the universe, God, your source, your guides or your higher self do not want you to take action right now.

Taking action is a big shift to make and it makes all the difference. Your higher self or whatever you choose to call it wants for you whatever you want for yourself. If you desire it, it is possible. It is part of why you are here.

Change Your Perspective

Realize that when your stuff comes up, it means you are doing the work to achieve your dream. Just beyond this part of the process is the gold, the life, the success, the freedom and the release you are seeking.

Looking at it this way reframes it. You can avoid going into crisis when this happens by realizing it is part of the process. Now you can work with it and use it as a catalyst for your personal and spiritual growth and development.

You have a feeling-guidance system within you. When you step up and say, "I am successful, I'm a business person, I am going to be more, have more, and do more" you are telling the universe you are ready to be used. Expect the universe to respond in a big way.

Intention

When you have something showing up in your life, it always started with an intention. That's great, if you have been consciously creating, but not always so much if you have been unconsciously creating.

It starts with desire. You have a desire and set an intention. You are always setting intentions, either consciously or unconsciously. What you ask for and what you believe and expect shows up all around you.

When a client comes to me with something she does not want showing up in her life, I go back to when it first occurred to discover what she asked for. It could have been a conscious or an unconscious request. We can always find a starting point that first brought the energy of this into physical form.

The key is to become more and more conscious about setting intentions. Get clarity and become centered, focused and grounded. The number one thing that people come to me with is confusion. Therefore, your first step is to transform your confusion into clarity. Whatever you are asking, the universe is answering. Remaining in a state of confusion is a choice. If you stay in a confused state for any length of time, you are choosing that, and it is serving you.

You are refusing to see or respond to something. Go back and take honest inventory and figure out why you need to stay in this state. Then take steps to move into clarity. When faced with confusion, you can always do something to move out of it.

Take 100 percent responsibility to push through your confusion. Recognize it as resistance. Wherever there is a need and a desire, there is also the ability to fulfill it. Now.

Opportunity

There is always a way forward from wherever you now stand.

When you set an intention, you activate *Ask and it is given*. Every sacred text has a version of this. However, many people no longer believe it is true. Even though it happens every day, you may not understand it, and therefore you cannot see it and use it.

The moment you ask, it is given. Become hyper-alert and watch for what shows up—opportunity. It is up to you to see it and step into it. It does not always show up as you expect it to and it may not be comfortable. It will stretch you.

This discomfort and stretching is because you are asking for something you do not currently have. It is not in your environment because you are not yet a match for it. However, you have desire for it, therefore it is in your energy. You must bring it into physical form. You need to change something within yourself for it to show up outside of you. If you could already possess it, you would.

Do not get stuck here! A lot of people do. I urge you not to misread what is showing up first as a sign you are not supposed to have what you desire, or believe it is not time, or that it is not right for you. Spirit wants for you what you want for yourself. Spirit created you to be a creator and gave you free will. It is all here for you. You must choose it. Choose to be it, do it and have it.

As you seek to align yourself to what you desire, what shows up first can feel and look like a lot of crap. You are seeing everything that is not currently in alignment energetically with what you want to bring in. The universe is saying you can have what you want, however here is what you must release or deal with first.

When you see opportunity show up, stay with it. Hold space for what you want. Focus your will and stay the course. Here is another place where you might feel frustrated. Self-doubt can kick in. I encourage you not to turn away from what you are bringing in, because then you get into start and stop energy and what you desire stops moving toward you.

When that opportunity shows up, you want to meet it head on. Step up and take action. That is when you see the results and what you desire begins to show up in your world.

Action

Make a decision. It all starts right here. As soon as you do, you will set things in motion, and the Universe will conspire on your behalf. You have to take the first step. Every time.

Right after I created the body of work I call *Master the Art of Taking Action,* I had the opportunity to speak with Janet Switzer, business coach to Jack Canfield and many other well-known transformational leaders in the Human Potential Movement. As I was pitching her the work I was developing, she said, "I see what you do. Your message to people is, 'Get over your garbage and take action!'" Yes!

When I talk about my work, I talk about how to master the art of taking action so you can get moving in the direction of your dreams and desires and create a better life now. I got from where I was to where I am now by learning how to get over my garbage. Then I had to learn how to take action in an empowered and intuitive way that best serves me. I want the same for you, and I want it now! Do you?

People like you show up as my clients and students, beginning to make new discoveries about themselves and their world and creating powerful shifts in their thoughts, feelings and beliefs. Yet, they are still stuck right at the point where it is time to take action. Can you relate?

Along this journey, here are some of the things I did that you can do, too:
- Dig deep.
- Chip away at the crap.
- Build belief.
- Take massive action—consistently.
- Reclaim your divine birth right.
- Embrace your purpose.
- Reframe everything.
- Invest in yourself through teachers, mentors, coaches and spiritual advisors.
- Allow the shift to happen.
- Up-level your environments.
- Connect with your passions and purpose and allow yourself the creative expression to integrate them into your everyday life.
- Be courageous enough to work on your emotional authenticity.

- Get clear with your money.
- Take honest inventory.
- Heal your issues that show up around your value, worth, gifts, self-image, need to be liked and self-promotion.
- Learn to manage your energy.
- Develop your intuition.
- Master your mindset.
- Recognize resistance and don't back down.
- Love yourself.

As you clear away more and more of the mental and emotional clutter that can overtake your life and block you from your connection to your inspiration, you will discover, as I did, that you can create a better life now. Get over your garbage. Get over the constant beating up and second-guessing and sabotaging yourself. Get over feeling that you are not enough.

You are here, now, and who you are is enough for someone. Your journey is important, and it can have an impact on others only when you are willing to share it. The best part is that sharing it is what brings you the most reward—mentally, physically, emotionally, spiritually and financially!

These are all a part of the process to master the art of taking action. This is what I work on with my clients and students as I continue to work on it in my own life. It has been life-changing and game-changing for me, and it absolutely can be for you, too. My life now is unrecognizable from the life I was living just five years ago.

If you are ready to create a better life now, I encourage you to make a decision to do so. Next, set a conscious intention based on something you desire. Immediately, begin watching for an opportunity to show up. When it does, take action.

Michelle Barr, MEd
Powerfully Practical and Spiritually Rich Tools for Creating A Better Life Now!

214-504-8610
michelle@michellebarr.com
www.theartoftakingaction.com

Michelle serves both her local community and a global clientele from her home in North Texas. She is a healer to healers and a leader to leaders. Michelle is a spiritual teacher, coach, mentor and guide for entrepreneurs who realize that their journey is one of personal and spiritual growth and development as well as business growth and development.

Michelle has a master's degree in counseling and guidance. She worked for many years as a mental health professional and crisis and trauma response specialist. In addition, she has training and experience as a hospital chaplain and an ordination as an interfaith minister.

Michelle serves her clients best by meeting them where they are and has created programs, products and services for her conscious clients looking to create both success and significance. She is a master healer and an energy medicine specialist trained and certified in many alternative and complementary healing modalities. Michelle's overall training, education, and experience has made her a personal transformation specialist. She serves her clients and students holistically, so they truly can create a better life now.

Trust the Experience

By Jadwiga Pylak

Coming from Poland to the United States in the 1970's was a difficult transition. I had to leave my family and friends. I was married within three months of my arrival to this new world. While establishing a family and a new life in America, I had to overcome a significant language barrier. Simply living in the country was not enough to assimilate. I had to take active steps to open myself to this new culture. I attended English classes and began making new friends.

Any immigrant will tell you that it takes time to become fluent in the language of a new home country. It was difficult for me to find a job because the language barrier was obvious during my interviews. After eight months of searching, I became frustrated. I decided to go into an interview for a job in the pharmaceutical industry and pretend that I understood English perfectly. This was quickly dispelled when the gentleman interviewing me asked, "How old are you?" and I replied, "I'm fine, thank you." As luck would have it, the interviewer was so amused by my guts to endure an entire interview in this way that he laughed and decided to hire me on the spot. Finally!

After being given this opportunity, I improved my language skills and was finally able to make friends and made my new country a place I could really call home. Within two years of being married, I had my first child, my son Artur. Twenty months later, I had my second child, my daughter Joanna. Somewhere in between juggling my work life and my growing family, I started doing energy readings for friends and colleagues.

I have always had unexplainable out-of-body experiences, a feeling of being in two places at the same time, and receiving information or premonitions. I have shared these gifts with others since childhood. After changing jobs in 1981 into the health care field, my social circle expanded and more and more people wanted to have energy readings done for them. They also asked for advice on their problems.

Understanding My Purpose

I became friends with a psychiatrist whom I asked for advice. He had witnessed my energy reading skills first-hand and suggested that I find someone who knew about metaphysics. As if the universe heard his advice, one of my good friends told me about a metaphysicist named Flo. My friend arranged an introduction. When I arrived for a session with her, Flo smiled at me and immediately knew that my intent of coming to her was to learn more about myself. During our three-hour session, she validated and clarified the experiences I was having with premonitions, which up to that point I had been harnessing by practicing energy readings with cards.

Flo explained to me that all humans are intuitive by nature. Some-where along the way as we leave childhood and move into adulthood, many of us push this intuition away. We become focused on the immediate, tangible or "seen" world around us as opposed to the spiritual or "unseen" energies around us. This intuition is there to guide and provide us with the information we need to connect with each other and ourselves on a deeper soul level. In my case, rather than pushing away this side of my humanity as I grew up, I had embraced and developed it.

Flo later became known as Flo Aeveia Magdalena, an author and channeler. However, from the day of our first meeting, she became my mentor and friend. Flo helped me to reach a deeper understanding of my spiritual life's purpose—to help people live from inside out, or perhaps more accurately, from "insight" out.

What does living from inside out—or "insight" out—mean? Simply put, it means to live in peace. While we may know the definition of peace, it has become increasingly difficult for us to truly experience it, and even more difficult for us to act it out. From coming to terms with our childhoods, bullying and relationships to experiencing jealousy and judging one another, circumstances in our lives are continuously disconnecting us from ourselves. As a result, they take us further away from the peace that we so need.

We take on so much work and so many restless feelings. Without knowing how to shift, move and balance the energies in our bodies, we create stress, depression, substance abuse habits and even physical illnesses. We have become victims of the past. We relive past pains in the present and struggle to cope. We do not know how to move forward. We forget who we are.

With each passing day in this restless limbo, we add another brick to the ever-growing walls we create around ourselves. You would not know it by looking, because we spend most of the time running away from problems and pretending everything is fine.

I saw this aspect of the human condition more clearly while studying holistic principles in 1990's. I learned to look at the human body as being comprised of energy and to understand how this energy works.

I learned to recognize physical, emotional, mental and spiritual energy levels and how those levels can affect each other.

The energy levels the average human being utilizes are only the physical, emotional and mental. This leaves the spiritual level lacking. On a daily basis we acknowledge our physical levels by experiencing our physical senses: sight, sound, touch, smell and taste. We acknowledge our emotional levels by feeling happy or sad—along with the many other variations of emotions that are present simultaneously. When things in our lives go wrong, or even when they go right, our brains start to work overtime. Our natural tendency is to get stuck in our mental levels, locking ourselves in cocoons inside our heads and forgetting about our spiritual, or higher selves, completely.

You can reach the spiritual level within you through meditation. This may take the form of prayer, religious faith or holistic practices, whatever you choose to believe and feel is best for you. Through these means, we can connect with our higher selves and with the memory of peace that we have carried within us since the day we were born.

Forgive and Live

In the late 1990's, a woman I will call Grace, came for a one-on-one session with me after her friend had suggested it. While engaging in conversation with her, I learned she was the mother of three children and had experienced a few horrible tragedies. She, her husband and children immigrated to the United States in late '80's. A few years after relocating, Grace lost both her daughter and her husband in unexpected ways. Her daughter had gone to a nearby park to go jogging and never returned home. Grace received a call from the police telling her that her daughter had been shot in the head. Nine months later, she lost her husband. While he was swimming in the ocean, he had a heart attack and drowned.

When Grace told me this, I felt chills all over my body. I felt her pain and grief—or rather empathized, as such pain is unimaginable unless it happens to you first hand. I wondered how much more pain anyone could take.

Grace felt trapped, powerless and unable to move away from her sorrow. She told me that she thought her life had come to an end. Grace described suffering with, "Tears, depression, grief, loneliness, anger, pain, not sleeping at night, not trusting my life process any more, not knowing what would come next, not having other family members living in this country and a language barrier at that time. I didn't know how I would survive with my two other children who needed me more than ever."

I introduced Grace to meditation and energy healing. This has opened her to her higher self and she trusts her life process again. She has released her anger, pain and stress. Grace feels reconnected with unconditional love and inner peace. She has been able to forgive her daughter's killer. Grace says, "Connecting with the spiritual level helped me to discover a new world, a world of oneness and peace." For Grace to be able to say that she forgives the man who killed her daughter is a huge healing process. I believe it makes Grace a hero.

The Power to Heal

At the start of 2000, while teaching meditation and energy healing classes at the Wellness Connection Center at a local hospital, a woman I will call Dorothy, came to her first day of class crying. While hugging and comforting her, she confided in me that she had a late stage of cancer and wanted to at least stay alive long enough to attend her son's wedding. At that moment, I imaged Dorothy dancing at the wedding and that I was dancing in a circle with her. I spontaneously shared that image with her. Dorothy confided that her cancer was serious and treatment options were exhausted. Doctors had given her only six months to live and her son's wedding was 18 months away.

At that moment, I froze. I questioned myself about whether I should have shared with her the image I saw. Dorothy asked me again if I really saw her dancing at her son's wedding and my answer was yes. From deep inside, I trusted my vision. Opening completely to holistic healing, trusting, believing, finding inner peace and accepting sickness, Dorothy certainly lived to be at her son's wedding and managed to stay on earth a little longer—three years beyond the original prognosis!

Dorothy gave me permission to share her thoughts from a letter she wrote to me before her passing. She told me that she had struggled with depression and fear as she battled her rare and deadly cancer. Dorothy did not want to give up when her doctor concluded that they had tried everything possible. She had already endured six different chemotherapies and two radiation therapies. With a strong desire to be there for her son's wedding, she decided to try alternative therapies.

Meditation and energy healing showed Dorothy a whole new world that gave her hope. She told me that she discovered a spiritual side of herself she had been ignoring. Dorothy learned that she had the power to heal herself and change the course of her disease. She wrote, "I was able to witness my son's wedding and was also able to dance all night long. I knew that a 'miracle' was happening on that day. Science told me I would not make it to the wedding, but I did."

Dorothy said that she went from having a cynical, pessimistic and suspicious outlook to having a heightened awareness of the world's beauty and the inherent goodness in people. Throughout her illness,

Dorothy observed so much good in people that she wondered why world peace is so difficult to attain.

Taking the First Step

A woman I will call Micky is the mother of three children. I met her at the end of 2003, when she was addicted to drugs, alcohol and cigarettes. Micky had reached a point where her addictive habits were out of control. Everything came to a climax when she almost set her house on fire. Her husband came home from work that day in time to contain the blaze before it could cause major damage.

For Micky, this near tragedy and the guilt of having come close to causing harm to her children and herself was a wakeup call. She admitted herself to a rehabilitation clinic. With a combination of therapies including counseling, Alcoholics Anonymous and meditation energy healing, Micky turned her life around. She addressed the underlying issues that lead to her addictions and has become a stronger, more positive person.

Now Micky shares her message with others. "Don't allow addiction to control you, do not wait for tragedy to happen, it's never too late to reach for help and reconnect with your spiritual self to bring what is the best of you into the world."

The truth is, we do not need a major crisis or tragedy to push us to live inside out. We are capable of it now, right this very second. We just need to trust the experience and take the first step.

In order to heal, take time to meditate and heal your old wounds. This might be difficult at first, however it becomes easier with time.
• Concentrate and look for the positive in every aspect of your life.
• Create an intention for peace and live in the moment.

- Look at the experience as something from which you can learn.
- Forgive others and yourself.
- Embrace the experience as the best teacher in your life.

Your experiences have helped you to be who you are today and will continue to help you grow. Believe that there is a reason behind every experience you have. If you continue this daily and try to disconnect with all the negative thoughts that hold you back, your life will change and the world will be a better place to live.

Jadwiga Pylak

Inner Wisdom & Energy Enlightenment LLC
It is not about changing your life...
it's about reconnecting with inner peace...
860-436-9409
jadwiga_pylak@yahoo.com
www.meditationandpeace.com

Jadwiga "Hedy" is a naturally gifted visionary, healer and inspirational community leader. Born in Poland, she first realized her gift for visualization as a child. Since moving to the United States in 1975, Hedy continued to develop herself as a visionary and energy reader and as a holistic practitioner. She found holistic healing work to be her life's destiny given her interest in people and compassion for helping others.

Hedy offers people a unique combination of energy readings, meditation coaching and energy healing sessions. She also leads and facilitates numerous workshops on holistic practices. Throughout more than forty years of holistic service, Hedy has touched thousands of lives serving people from all walks of life and mentored other healers. Her true passion is assisting others to find inner connection.

Hedy is the founder of Inner Wisdom & Energy Enlightenment LLC and is on the Board of Directors of Soul Support Systems. She is also a hypnotherapist certified by the Hypnosis International Board of Registration and Shift Network Certified Peace Ambassador. She lives in Newington, Connecticut with her loving family.

Persistence Pays

Do Not Give Up on Your Dreams

By Angeli Raven Fitch, Esq.

*L*ife would be so much easier if we could just achieve our goals and dreams effortlessly and without failing. It would be like winning the lottery! You would be able to simply snap your fingers to have whatever you strongly desired. No struggling, no failing, no rejection and no pain.

I would be willing to bet that no one has truly gone after his or her dreams and not failed. After all, McDonald's founder Raymond Kroc failed over and over again before McDonald's became the huge empire it is today. Mr. Kroc believed that failure was an important teacher and catalyst for success. When asked about how luck played into the McDonald's success, he said, "Luck is a dividend of sweat. The more you sweat, the luckier you get." What set him apart from others was his "bounce back" ability. Each time he fell, he bounced back and kept going.

One of the most important qualities a successful person can have is persistence. Persistence is an attitude of never giving up, especially when times are tough. I have learned to see each of my failures as an opportunity for growth. Instead of wallowing in my failures and feeling sorry for myself, I now acknowledge the disappointment, dust myself off and get right back up. Failure now is a welcome part of my journey.

Bishop T.D. Jakes, best-selling author and the founder and pastor of The Potter's House, said, "A setback is a set up for a comeback." This is one of my favorite quotes because it reminds me that failure can be a great motivator in success. What if you actually embraced failure and looked at it as a gift? I invite you to change your relationship with failure. Success is right around the corner.

> *"It is not how many times you fall down,*
> *it is how many times you get back up!"*
> **—Author Unknown**

Many years ago, I almost gave up on my dream of being an attorney. I had a fantastic experience in law school and looked forward to a career as a criminal defense attorney. However, there was one final obstacle in the way, passing the California Bar Exam!

Right after graduation, and for the next three months, my law school friends and I panicked to cram all twelve subjects of the law into our brains. We took the exam that summer and then had to wait a grueling four months for the results. They would be posted online on the State Bar website at exactly 6 p.m. on a Friday evening. My friends and I gathered anxiously to see our fate. Who was going to pass? Who was going to fail? As each of my friends screamed in excitement about their name showing up on the pass list, I sat still frozen in shock. No matter how many times I put my bar exam number on the website, my name refused to come up!

I felt sick to my stomach with embarrassment and shame. My heart sank and my spirit sank even deeper. This was truly the first time in my life that I failed at something for which I had a burning desire. Failure was not an option. I had never even considered the possibility of failure.

What I did not know at the time was this was only the beginning of a long journey of failing the exam several more times. Statistics showed that each time a person failed the exam, the chances that he or she would eventually pass decreased significantly. Not only was failure an option, it was a highly likely outcome! The odds were against me and even my family members were encouraging me to give up. I was at a very low point and felt alone with my failure.

Persistence Changed My Life

My journey of failure with the bar exam lasted three long years—the same amount of time it took me to complete law school. The key to my not giving up was that each time I failed, I reconnected to my mission and vision of why I wanted to become an attorney in the first place. What was the "soul" of my dream to become an attorney? Why did it matter to me so much? This gave me the strength I needed to persist and not give up.

A major turning point for me occurred during the sixth and final time I took the exam. On the first day of the exam, I took some time to meditate and to connect to my wiser inner voice. That voice told me to focus on what I wanted to contribute to society in my work as an attorney. The exam was not about me. Someone in jail or prison needed what I had to offer. Someone innocent was rotting away in prison and needed me to pass this exam. Wow! This was not about what I was going to get personally, it was about what I was going to give. It was about the contribution I was going to make to society and how that filled me with so much hope, desire, excitement and passion. My persistence led me to the realization that it did not matter if I failed again this time. I was going to take the exam as many times as it took for me to become the attorney I was meant to be.

I cannot imagine not being an attorney. It brings tears to my eyes when I think of how my journey of failure was really an incredible journey of self-realization. To be credible and trustworthy in your own eyes is powerful stuff!

I now had a track record of success on my own terms. Today I work with many people who represent a forgotten segment of the population—the mentally ill, the falsely accused and the poor. What my clients can count on is that because of my persistence, I will not give up on them. I look at failure in a totally different way. Persistence pays. Never give up on your dreams.

How to Turn Failure into Success

I used several strategies that significantly helped me during the tough times when giving up on my dreams would have been so much easier. You can take action with all these strategies.

- Create or revisit your vision and mission statements.
- Create a vision board to help manifest your dreams.
- Read personal development or personal growth books.
- Hire a business coach to hold you accountable.
- Keep a gratitude journal and quit feeling sorry for yourself.
- Meditate daily or spend time in quiet contemplation.
- Exercise at least three days a week and play like a joyful kid again!

Write Vision and Mission Statements

Do you know where you are going and what your purpose is? Many people confuse the vision statement with the mission statement. Your vision is a statement of where you or your company are going. Your mission is a statement of how you will accomplish your vision.

> *"If you don't know where you are going,*
> *how will you know when you get there?"*
> **—Julie Morgenstern, American author, speaker**
> **and time management expert**

Some people prefer to create the vision statement first or vise versa. It really does not matter which one you complete first, as long as there is a strong connection that gives you inspiration and direction. I suggest you read your vision and mission statements aloud every morning. Making a declaration every day gives you the inspiration and direction you need to keep you grounded and strong.

Create a Vision Board

Most of us are very visual when it comes to accomplishing our goals. I recommend scheduling a whole day for creating your vision board. Accumulate a stack of magazines and newspapers in which you can choose visual images that match your vision or mission. Do not spend too much time thinking about choosing the right or perfect picture, just let your mind run free and choose what feels right. It may take many months later for your mind to catch up with your intuition as to why you chose that image. You can make it extra fun by getting together with a group of like-minded dreamers. (See Nora Cabrera's chapter, The Universe Is Within You on page 33 and Linda Ballesteros' chapter, The Secret to Finding Your Bliss on page 11)

I created my first vision board twenty years ago when I was in my twenties. I have since created many vision boards and I love to see how my goals and dreams have changed and evolved. The vision board inspires and excites the imagination. The more you look at it, the more your mind figures out how to make these images turn into physical reality.

Spend Time Reading

I love to read positive, uplifting books about how ordinary people overcame life's struggles and challenges. During the tough times, I found it very impactful to sit down with a good book that inspired me to keep going. The autobiography of Helen Keller was an especially inspiring story that taught me about persistence and courage. Make sure you have several books on your bookshelf to keep you motivated.

Hire a Business Coach

We all need help in accomplishing our goals. One of the things I learned early is that I cannot hold myself accountable 100 percent of the time. It is too easy to let yourself off the hook. I have made countless to do lists only to make excuses for myself as to why I could not complete the tasks I set out to do. One of the best decisions I made was to hire a business coach, Crystal Shanks of Action Coach, to keep me on track on a weekly basis. If I knew I had to answer to Crystal, it gave me an extra incentive not to let her down. Sometimes we are much better at keeping promises to others than we are to ourselves.

Keep a Gratitude Journal

Instead of drowning in your sorrows, shift the attention to all that you have now. You have so much to be grateful for. This was a challenging exercise for me to do at first. I resisted because I did not understand what this had to do with achieving my goals.

I started out slow and chose to write one thing every morning for which I was grateful. This was a profound exercise. The most amazing thing happened to me throughout my day. Every time something difficult or challenging came up, I would have an instant flashback about what I wrote in my journal that morning.

One day, I was rejected by a client who chose a much more experienced and well-known attorney over me. In that moment, I was filled with gratitude. I thought, *Well, at least I get to go home to a man who loves me no matter what.* Ah, life was not so bad.

Put your gratitude journal in your living room and write something in it every day. At the end of the year, on New Year's Eve, you have a beautiful ritual to experience—a celebration of all you were grateful for throughout the year.

Meditate Daily

It is during our quiet times that we can really hear the wisdom that is always there and wants to speak to us. In the beginning, I had so much trouble sitting quiet and doing nothing. I hated it, to say the least. At first, you can try this for a few minutes every day. Sit in silence or play a guided meditation tape. The important thing is that you make time each day to sit quietly and do nothing. This is a learned skill. It takes focus and discipline. (see Tammy Phye's chapter, Tragedy to Thriving on page 129)

Schedule Exercise

Handling the responsibilities of daily life or owning your own business can cause an incredible amount of stress–emotionally, mentally and physically. You can take time out to meditate, relax or talk to a therapist. However, if your body is not in alignment to deal with the stress, you may seek other ways of coping. For some people, this means overindulging in alcohol, drugs or food. One of the best decisions I made to alleviate stress was to quit smoking and take up tennis to replace it. I absolutely fell in love with playing tennis and to this day, I play at least three to four days a week. Find a form of exercise that you really enjoy and can incorporate into your daily lifestyle. (see Dr. Yvette Nadeau's chapter, Achieving Health and Vitality in Your Life on page 109)

Do Not Give Up on Your Dreams, Take Action Now!

It is important to begin these strategies as soon as possible if you want to achieve your dreams. Assume that you will hit some bumpy roads as you move toward your dream. There is no easy and painless way of getting what you want.

The starting point is asking yourself, *What is my dream? What do I want out of life?* This will lead you to your vision and mission statements. Rather than listing all your dreams, focus on just one. It can be a career dream or a personal dream. For example, maybe you want to start your own business or you want to start a family. What is that one dream burning inside you? Internalize the depth of what that dream means to you. This keeps you going through the tough times when it seems so much easier to give up.

We are all talented and unique. However, only the strong among us survive. Persistence pays. Do not give up on your dreams!

Angeli Raven Fitch, Esq.
Your freedom is my business

415-913-7742
angeli@fitchcriminaldefense.com
www.fitchcriminaldefense.com
www.threestrikesjusticecenter.com

Angeli R. Fitch is a highly skilled criminal defense attorney in private practice in the San Francisco Bay Area. She is a passionate advocate for all her clients and believes in the presumption of innocence— one is innocent until proven guilty. Angeli is particularly sensitive to issues facing the mentally ill, the wrongfully convicted and inmates on death row.

Angeli manages Fitch Criminal Defense PC, a firm committed to making a positive social impact in today's challenging criminal justice system. While the traditional approach focuses solely on defending a client based on a legal analysis of the facts and law, Angeli's firm practices "holistic" criminal defense and sees the client as a person who is part of a larger community. Angeli's upcoming book *Holistic Justice–Getting to the Heart of the Matter* will be a guide for attorneys to bring emotional intelligence into their relationships with clients.

Angeli is also a founding partner with the Three Strikes Justice Center, LLP, a law firm dedicated to helping inmates transition out of the prison system because of their eligibility for resentencing and a new life.

Lead Life Now... Not Tomorrow

By Paula-Jo Husack, MA, LMFT, CGP

*Y*ou have launched a life-developing commitment by reading this book. You are on a bridge, going from where you are to where you want to be. This chapter introduces you to a life leadership approach called LeadLifeNow©. You can learn to be your own leader in the personal and professional areas that make up your whole life design.

How do you become a leader? It takes desire, determination, patience and pursuit of your own retraining. We call it "brain training," although your whole heart comes along, too. Our inefficient habits continue with existing patterns of thoughts, actions, emotions (feelings), and physical sensations (feelings).

Building and sustaining awareness of these patterns is next. At first, you may become aware after the fact. This is still use of your awareness tool. Clients, who are accustomed to achieving quickly and well, are disappointed after a few weeks of noticing after the fact. Ask yourself, "How long have I been doing the patterns of disservice?" One year? Forty years? Each year holds your patterns in place more strongly. Fortunately, women have retrained their brains even after sixty years!

Determination and practice, practice, practice cracks the cement! Give your brain time to reroute. Become aware. With practice you develop new, empowering patterns. An actual brain scan would show the presence of new, thin "threads"—actual neural pathways of new habits. As your new patterns become more prevalent, these "threads" will show bolder in future scans.

How do you develop new patterns? Give conscious attention to the life elements listed in this chapter. Gather meaningful pictures, photos and quotations that represent what you want in each life element. Create a vision book or vision board with these elements. Post inspirational quotes near your desk, in your car or in your bathroom. Listen to song lyrics that say what you want. These are your personalized icons in this journey toward true wholeness and optimal performance. Simultaneously, you are training your brain in positive change and in LeadLifeNow leadership. Your focus moves from depleting actions to completing actions.

These are short- and long-term goals. Take solid steps to regard, review and manage these essential, whole-life fundamentals. This means no longer putting them aside or reactively responding to the world happening to you. It means stepping through a planning process for each project that includes all your thoughts, emotions, physical sensations and resulting actions.

"It's not the load that breaks you down, but the way you carry it."
—Lena Horne, American singer, actress, dancer and Civil Rights activist

With deliberate attention, you build and maintain a solid personal and professional life foundation. On this, you can develop, launch and sustain your goals and dreams. Everyone needs a well-designed, well-maintained foundation on which to build her life's castle.

Position that castle for whole-kingdom governance. When it runs well, you have more time for pleasure!

You can start now, wherever you are. Your environment is not the predictor. Your internal environment—self-regard, desire and motivation—is.

Have you ever wanted your environment "just so" before proceeding with a plan? Environment does not necessarily predict an outcome. I have seen this when teaching self esteem-building classes. I witnessed some awesome individuals who won over a negative daily setting. I saw their core optimism, hope and will to build self-esteem.

Let's compare two groups of people I worked with in very different environments. The first, I call the San Francisco group. It was made up of men of all ages, cultures and backgrounds. They lived in a temporary residence—the San Francisco County Jail.

In contrast, the group I call the Peninsula group was made up of women of all ages, cultures and backgrounds. They lived in long-term housing. It was suburban private-practice land of residential houses, yards, condos and apartment buildings.

At first, you would think the two groups were very different. However, they were more similar than you might imagine. There were some differences, like their bedrooms, dinner plates and meeting spaces. The jail offered a large, vacant holding cell without heat, where I taught our self-esteem-building classes. Private-practice land was a comfortable, living room-like office.

More important were the similarities. Both groups were culturally diverse, had no previous training in functional life leadership and lived with a high level of stress. Their behavioral patterns were repetitive and inefficient. However, they had core seeds of optimism: strong spiritual and humanistic beliefs, an openness and willingness to change, and voluntary commitment.

Do you recognize any of their similarities in yourself? You bring these mindsets to your journey of life leadership. That journey begins now, wherever you are. You are the leader of your whole life. Your approach empowers your leadership.

Here are the 14 primary life elements of the LeadLifeNow model.

1. Environment—personal spaces, such as home, car or office

2. Family of origin—the one into which you were born

3. Extended family—through marriage or partnership

4. Family of choice—the one you have created

5. Finance/money

6. Individuality/autonomy

7. Job/career

8. Love and intimacy

9. Parenting

10. Physical—health, diet, exercise

11. Purpose—life meaning

12. Sexuality

13. Social

14. Spiritual

Each is its own sphere, or life circle. Perhaps there are other circles of significance in your whole life. Take the time to know them, as they make up your own unique whole-person, whole-life design. Which circles need attention now?

Enter LeadLifeNow's circular model. Look at diagram A. This is the LeadLifeNow circular leadership model for getting things done. Compare it to the linear approach in diagram B, with which you may be more familiar. We learn the linear model from our school beginnings, for example, pass, fail and top-of-the-class. We know it in work, with project management. The starting point is on the left and the ending point, or goal, is on the right. You invest your efforts on the end goal—the finish line. You give yourself little personal acclaim along the way. In this approach, you just get to the finish line and move forward.

Take a look at the next linear model of personal performance, diagram C. The lines are connected at the top like a triangle. You aim for the top, or the peak. You have no regular, positive check-

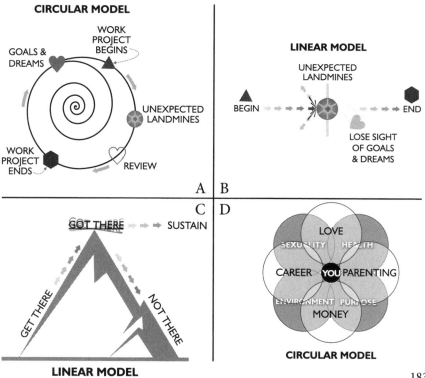

ins as you ascend the steps. This approach drives you to get to the top. However, when you finally reach your goal, you may have a problem. Climbers who arrive at the peak through the all-or-nothing model find that after a brief spectacular adrenaline high, there is nowhere to go except down. It is a steep, emotional and mental slide to the bottom.

> *"My grandfather once told me that there are two kinds of people: those who work and those who take the credit. He told me to try to be in the first group; there was less competition there."*
> **—Indira Ghandi, first woman prime minister of India**

When you work to LeadLifeNow, you gain from your efforts. The LeadLifeNow circular model has no severe ups and downs and no single straightaway from beginning to end. Each fundamental is its own circle within your life. You are at the center leading the way, like in diagram D. Sometimes these life circles intersect like the elements of life. What you do in your social sphere may impact your financial sphere. Your financial sphere may impact your love relationship plans or your career moves. Your family of choice may influence your extended family sphere. Each sphere influences others in different degrees at different times.

A circular model connotes movement like real life. There is no end point, only pause. For example, take the career circle. When you land a job position you want, the positive momentum continues with happiness, excitement and physical relief. You think, Awesome! Then new-employee learning, team expectation, tactics and satisfaction follow. Productivity and performance steps are also plotted on the circle. Your whole experience is noted. You manage with awareness and skill. You tune in to your actions, thoughts, emotions and physical sensations. This is a whole-person, whole-life approach. Like your life, the circle concept creates a moving, breathing dynamic. Hopefully, after this mini-intensive training, you are breathing too.

Each life circle views your conscious awareness. It is like governing your life through a wide-angle lens rather than a narrow-scoped telephoto lens. You execute movement and pause within each life fundamental. You lead because you are clear-minded, clear-sighted and proactive. With time and practice, you are also skilled. The process is yours.

The Inner Partner

Hundreds of women in LeadLifeNow workshops say their self-esteem hits the wall with the classic and contemporary linear models. When progress along that straight line halts, they feel anxiety or freeze. They have no view of what to do next. They have no skills for self-comfort or self-encouragement. Their inner judge's voice distracts and detracts from the fluid process. It is inhibiting, harsh, critical, blaming and perfectionistic. The judge is a common presence to those who work life on the linear model.

With the LeadLifeNow circular model, the inner judge's voice eventually quiets. The inner partner's voice awakens in the spirit of camaraderie, support, optimism and safety. As you practice, this assured voice ultimately takes the lead.

"I'm not afraid of storms, for I'm learning to sail my ship."
—Louisa May Alcott, American novelist

By the end of LeadLifeNow training, women learn that if a project freezes, they do not need to freeze. They replace the word "freeze" with "pause". They can plan what happens next with their eyes, ears and minds wide open—a learned clear, conscious thought process. They can plot their steps on a curved continuum and the circle never ends.

By now, you have already developed a leadership style within each of your LeadLifeNow circles. Is it proactive, reactive or both? It is like a mosaic. Take a minute now to piece together your leadership mosaic design:

Reactive

1. Finding problems and fixing them

2. Making decisions based on rules

3. Being the direction-giver

4. Controlling and fearing loss of control

5. Having your own answers

6. Making decisions alone

7. Pushing or pressuring for the outcome you want

8. Judging yourself and others

9. Maintaining a superior or inferior mindset

10. Expecting crisis

To understand yourself better, open your eyes wide to your reactive pieces. Do you choose them or do they exist because of another's influence, or both? Within what LeadlifeNow circles do they fit? Who makes your reactivity pop? When do you use your reactive pieces by choice? What patterns of thought, action or emotion keep these reactive pieces in place? How long have they been a part of this circle?

"It's better to look ahead and prepare, than to look back and regret."
—Jackie Joyner-Kersee, American Olympic gold medalist, philanthropist

Proactive

1. Anticipating the future

2. Gathering opinions before finalizing

3. Focusing on process steps and achievement results

4. Learning from and valuing errors

5. Seeing change as natural and influencing change for others

6. Sharing decision-making

7. Setting limits while staying flexible

8. Coaching yourself and others

9. Recognizing small rewards

10. Reviewing your wants and needs

11. Taking and sharing control for best results

Study your proactive mosaic pieces. Look back at the questions you asked yourself about your reactive mosaic and now ask them in relation to your proactive mosaic. Take your time. You may uncover valuable information. Singer Alicia Keys and designer Vera Wang have spent years learning and practicing their arts. They continue today! LeadLifeNow workshop participants train in their new "art" of the leadership model for weeks and master sustainable goals after many months and more. They keep it up and they tune-up. The circle model continues through life. Learning remains rich and enriches life.

"Make the most of yourself by fanning the tiny, inner sparks of possibility into flames of achievement."
—Golda Meir, Israel's first woman prime minister, teacher and kibbutznik

If you passionately desire to lead your life now, your greater vision must be about making and sustaining life change and plotting it on a circular continuum. It must be about risk-taking and listening to the quartet of your heart, head, soul and gut. At first, this can feel uncomfortable or produce anxiety. It is unfamiliar. Your body may physically flag you to stop by creating temporary shallow breaths, headaches, rapid heartbeats, irritable digestion or unhealthy cravings. If you are thrilled about the empowering possibilities, the brain will release happy chemicals, like endorphins. Your body may respond with a smile on your face that stretches the length of the Golden Gate Bridge.

Change is natural and organic. It is like the unfamiliarity with a new fitness routine or the difficulty of a beginning foreign language class. We are all in good company with Olympic athletes, top litigators, new parents, performing artists and first-graders. Body messages speak from the zones of transitional change. As you learn to lead your life now, watch your discomfort evolve into comfort and confidence. With time and training, your castle and kingdom develop a routine maintenance schedule. This ensures heat in the winter and tulips in the spring.

> *"You can't be that kid standing at the top of the waterslide, over thinking it. You have to go down the chute."*
> —**Tina Fey, American actor, comedian, writer and producer**

The LeadLifeNow process develops your awareness of thoughts, feelings, and sensations in partnership with actions and responses. When movement or change occurs within a life circle, you can choose your response. When there is calm and consistency, you can choose to enjoy the ride. When there is urgency, you can craft your response. The landscape of each circle becomes familiar. Plans, goals, dreams, and accomplishments live within each. You can see where the circles intersect.

Learn how your emotions and physical sensations produce the starts, stops and ultimate outcomes you want. Here is a taste of the LeadLifeNow process:

1. Choose one of your 14 fundamental circles. List significant people, events or things influencing its current status. Remember, one of them is you.

2. Physical awareness. Close your eyes and focus inward. Ask yourself, "Am I comfortable or uncomfortable when I focus on this circle? Where in my body do I feel this sensation" (for example, tight stomach, relaxed, blocked with no sensation, shallow breathing)?

3. Thoughts. What are they? Which voice speaks: the judge, the anxious child, the collaborative partner, the safe grown-up?

4. Emotions. (not to be confused with "being emotional") What emotions do you feel? Happiness, relief, excitement, fear?

5. Actions. What is a manageable move for today? If not today, when? Is it short- or long-term? Is pause the best tactic for now?

Now you have stepped through a mini-version of the LeadLifeNow leadership process. You have information on which to expand and to add to your self- esteem. Continue your commitment down the circular path. Transfer the linear segments. Enjoy the broad, deep, clear view of your life management and personal growth journey. Unite and grow your relationship with yourself, within and without. Keep connected with amazing mentors of the past, present and future. Keep a sense of humor. Pay attention to the whole sky throughout all your seasons. Learn the stars and their constellations. Stand strong, steady and skilled.

Be ready to catch your star again and again—with the biggest, boldest net.

Paula-Jo (PJ) Husack, MA, LMFT, CGP
Leadlifenow®
Coach, Counselor, Consultant,
Speaker, Author
650-619-6521
pj@leadlifenow.com
www.leadlifenow.com

Paula-Jo (PJ) is a native San Franciscan who lives a full, diverse life and serves others in optimizing theirs. PJ launched her private practice in the 1990's following corporate beginnings. Today she sees clients in her offices, their workplaces, stages, courtrooms and athletic venues.

PJ grew up valuing learning, creativity, music and emotional expression. She was influenced by her older sister's physical challenges, operatic voice and optimism. PJ's own life-threatening illness has led her to guide others in their own life leadership journey. She has an undergraduate degree in both media communications and counseling psychology and a graduate degree in counseling psychology. She is licensed in marriage and family therapy, certified in EMDR; and has a specialty in performance enhancement. PJ internationally presents her inspirational, down-to-earth and dynamic presentations on Mind Matters: Life Leadership Connections for healthcare workers, parents, and professional and personal organizations.

PJ enjoys her family, the arts and nature. She is a photo artist, cartoonist and supports the SFJazz mission. Find her performing with Joyce McBride's Conspiracy of Venus, a contemporary San Francisco women's acapella choir. PJ volunteers with the American Cancer Society and is a past board member.

Women and Power

Seven Energy Keys to Turn Lead Weight into Gold Power!

By Beverly Adamo, MA, CDC

*C*ongratulations on keeping your Divine Appointment to discover what lead weight is keeping you from the joy that is possible when you own and use your power!

> *"You are far more powerful than you realize.*
> *You are creating everything in your life.*
> *Once you fully acknowledge this and take responsibility*
> *for it, you can do anything that you set your mind to.*
> *You are the author of your own life*
> *and you can choose to take it any direction you wish."*
> **—Jack Canfield, American motivational speaker and author**

Women often wear their power rather than owning and using it. Unclaimed power becomes a weight that can keep you from joy. Whether the weight is physical, emotional, mental or all of the above, and whether it manifests as unhealthy pounds on your hips or unhealthy personal or business relationships, the Seven Energy Keys described in this chapter can immediately:

• Help you release excess weight
• Change lifelong eating patterns with ease
• Release old relationships

- Transform current relationships
- Upgrade your business and career

The possibilities are unlimited.

Energy Key #1: Your Story—Your Source Code

Your story is much more than just your biography or timeline. It is what you tell yourself and others about who you are and your life experiences. Interestingly, Your Story can be absolute truth and distorted perception. Usually, it is a combination of both. You experience the circumstances of your life through your mental *and* emotional filters. Capturing Your Story can provide you with a useful, powerful tool. Keep it in a computer file or notebook to easily reference. Start now and write whatever comes to you without judgment or editing. Just write!

As you travel along this path of power, more information about Your Story will come to you. Write it down! Taking Your Story out of your mental storage creates a vacuum for miracles to occur. The more information in Your Story, the richer this resource becomes for owning your power. Are you ready to transform?

1. Where are you "stuck" in your life? Do you continue to exhibit a behavior that does not serve you?

2. Ask Your Story, "What is the source of this issue?" and write your answer. The source is somewhere in Your Story, maybe even from before you were born—a past life. You may be surprised.

3. What can you transform about that source event, feeling or circumstance? Your perception? Your belief? Someone or something to forgive? Hint: remember to forgive yourself!

Celebrate using Your Story successfully as a powerful tool to transform your life.

Energy Key #2: Beliefs—the Power to Choose

Imagine your life if you believe:

- You deserve unlimited abundance simply because you are alive.
- You are healthy and fit, vibrant and beautiful, sexy and sensual, loving and loved.
- You are living the life of your dreams because you are a powerful, self-fulfilled woman.
- You choose your beliefs and are willing to exchange any that do not serve you for empowering beliefs.

The great news is that you do choose your beliefs. It is critical to understand that you may not have made these choices consciously. Some of the most debilitating beliefs are those you have unconsciously chosen and formed. That is what can make this Energy Key challenging. However, if you are willing to accept full responsibility—the ability to respond—for your beliefs, you can reclaim a major component of your power. You can catapult your ability to change your lead weight into gold power. Here is how:

1. Envision a book detailing all your beliefs. Clearly visualize it, including the space in which it resides.

2. Review Your Story and some of the unsuccessful behaviors you repeat. Ask yourself, "What would I have to believe about myself or my world, or about how things work, for me to do what I have done in my life?" For example, if you find yourself procrastinating, what would you have to believe in order to continue to do this? That you have to be perfect, that you are not good enough or that someone will laugh at you?

3. Change a limiting belief to an empowering belief. Obliterate the limiting belief. Visualize crossing it out with a black magic marker or ripping the page out of your book of beliefs. Burn it and bury the ashes. Then choose a clean page and write your empowering belief.

4. Think about what habits you need to clean up around that limiting belief. What personal power practices must you instill to support your empowering belief?

5. Your Story also contains empowering beliefs. Look at Your Story from that perspective and answer the question, "What would I have to believe about myself or my world, or how things work for me to have successfully accomplished what I have in my life?" Have fun with this question.

Remember, you are only a choice away from removing any limiting belief and installing your new empowering belief. Celebrate your successes and empowering beliefs.

Energy Key #3: Divine Configuration
You may have been told that ego is bad. The truth is that we are born with a Divine Configuration that is an equal balance of ego and spirit. Both are Divine. Ego is the manifesting machine and spirit provides the resources that make it work. What does that mean?

As far as SPIRIT is concerned, it is *all* good. SPIRIT is only one energy-in-motion (e-motion), and that is love. EGO on the other hand, provides us with the ability to think, which can result in e-motions like fear, doubt, disbelief, anger and so on. Your EGO gives you discernment and choice. You use your EGO to take action and choose what you want in your life, what you like and dislike, your goals and dreams.

Within the human system consisting of EGO and SPIRIT, only five to seven percent of your system exists within your consciousness. The remaining 93 to 95 percent is below the surface of your consciousness. Think of a time when you did something completely stupid or contrary to what you knew. When the majority of thoughts and beliefs exist in the unconscious, is it really any wonder that you find yourself asking, "Oh my God, what was I thinking?"

Now that you are aware how much goes on in the unconscious, must you expand your conscious mind? Not necessarily. Think about your miraculous body. So much of what occurs with it is on an unconscious level, thank goodness! Imagine having to think consciously about taking each breath, blinking or keeping your heart beating! Most of your manifestation can take place on an unconscious level as well.

NOTE: Be sure to align your unconscious dreams with your conscious dreams for your life. Here is how:

1. Think of a time when you asked yourself, "What the heck was I thinking?" Describe what happened in detail.

2. Refer to Your Story or ask yourself, "Where have I done this (or something like it) before?" What are the similarities in the experiences? What are the differences?

3. Identify any beliefs that would have to exist for you to behave or take the action you did. Use your tools to change any limiting beliefs.

4. Affirm what you want in your life through a written and compelling vision. Focus consistently on that vision to realign your unconscious and conscious.

Like a computer, you can "reboot" your human system and restore the Divine Configuration of balance between EGO and SPIRIT.

Energy Key #4: Creative Heart—Intuition
Your Creative Heart Intuition is the path of trusted communication between your SPIRIT and EGO. If you are not used to following your intuition, you can practice by asking a question, listening to the answer and following the guidance. For example, you might ask *I wonder where I left my keys?* Listen to the answer, *Under the bench*

in the garage. Even if you are in the habit of asking questions, if you ignore the guidance, *There is no way my keys could have ended up under the bench in the garage!* then your heart's path of intuition becomes cluttered with junk and gunk. It is time to clear the path of any junk, gunk and obstacles and restore clarity.

A tool you can use to clear and deepen your Creative Heart Intuition is Active Imagination. Start a dialogue with SPIRIT through your Intuition. Write down a question and write down the answer. Use the initial of your first name to represent you, and another initial to represent your Intuition. For example:

B: *I wonder, what do I need to know about my next step in business?*
I: *That you are over-thinking things. Talk to Janie about what you are doing. She has a connection for you.*

1. Suspend disbelief and judgment. Play with using your intuition by using the words, I wonder...

2. Listen to the answer. It may come in the form of a picture or words in your mind, or just a feeling of being drawn to someone or something in your life.

3. Deepen your connection with the unconscious through a daily practice of active imagination. *Hint:* Be sure to write these dialogues and then go back and read them later—your thoughts may amaze you!

4. Act on your intuition.

Discover how eager your SPIRIT is to share the abundant resource of information with you.

Energy Key #5: Physical Alchemy
You are a physical alchemist. You are creating in every moment and turning one physical substance into another. Your body converts

food to nutrients and energy you use for daily activities. You convert salary into your home, car, clothes, toys and so on. Because much of this manifestation is methodical and mundane, you may not truly recognize the fact that you are an alchemist...turning one substance into another.

Another way to create and manifest is through a magical and miraculous process. The next time you want a new car, instead of manifesting the car in a methodical and mundane manner— shopping, figuring out how to pay for it, worrying that you cannot afford it, making the choice and negotiating for it—you might try the magical and miraculous path instead. All it requires is for you to believe that you are entitled to miracles and can create magically. Why not? Here is how, using the new car as the example.

1. Start with what you desire.

2. Set your intention for what you desire. *Within three months, I own a (describe the car in detail), free and clear.*

3. Take action by noticing how often this car starts to "show up" in your life. It may be a picture, or the car ahead of you, or an ad on the radio. This is the Universe handling the details.

4. Remove any doubts or limiting beliefs you have around this intention and this process of manifestation.

5. Practice gratitude daily for all you receive—especially when you are driving your new car!

The difference between an intention and a goal is this: with an intention, you set it and allow the Universe to handle the details. Setting a goal requires you to take action. Physical alchemy requires both. As you become more comfortable with the fact that you create what you have in your life, you also learn to transmute any lead weight that exists in your life into useful power.

Energy Key #6: Your Unique Factor

You may have heard this called your purpose. Just like you...it is one of a kind. No one else has your Unique Factor. Awaken to it and live consciously. Know your Unique Factor and *everything* in your life will have purpose. You begin to live a ritual life...every moment transformed from ordinary into extraordinary. You become unstoppable!

If you do not know what Your Unique Factor is, just breathe! The truth is, every moment of your life is *on purpose.* The question is whether you are aware of that purpose. Every experience in Your Story provides information about Your Unique Factor. Here is a simple process to discover or deepen your understanding:

1. Imagine you have travelled forward in time ten years and you are celebrating and receiving an award for having changed the world.

2. Listen to what your family, friends, associates and mentors say about you as your best and most successful self. Write down the qualities they say you have.

3. Write down what they say you love to do.

4. Notice and write down what they say you accomplished, how you changed the world for the better.

5. Complete the following sentence: *My purpose is* (list one or two of the qualities from number two) *by* (list what you love to do from number three) *to* (what you have accomplished from number four).

6. The end result might look like this: *My purpose is to intuitively empower myself and others by creating and sharing our visions to awaken humanity, understanding spiritual truths and experiencing infinite abundance.*

Know that you cannot do this wrong. Your Unique Factor, the reason you are here is eagerly waiting to make itself known to you.

Energy Key #7: Possibility Code

Deepak Chopra speaks of the field of all possibilities. He teaches that at the highest level, you are a field of all possibilities. (see Tobey Allen's chapter, Master the Art of Possibilities on page 63) Your life as you now experience it is a reflection of your Possibility Code. Think of it as infinitely expanded DNA. If you are not living your dream life that is because of the possibilities you have chosen. Like your beliefs, you can choose different possibilities for your life if your current Possibility Code does not bring you complete joy. How do you rewrite your Possibility Code?

1. Give yourself the gift of time to define what your dream life looks like. Write about it in detail.

2. Allow your fear and doubt to surface. Identify your limiting beliefs and replace them.

3. What people, places or things do you need to let go of that no longer have a place in your dream life? Let them go.

4. Expand your dream further and identify what possibilities you will choose to live that dream. If you find yourself struggling with this process, work with a partner or coach.

Remember that you have the field of *all* possibilities from which to choose. Have fun!

Step Into Your Truth Now!

You are a powerful woman with the ability to transform lead weight in your life. Invest twenty minutes each day using these Energy Keys. You are worth it. Create your daily Power Ritual to own and use *your* golden power to *catch your star!*

Beverly Adamo, MA, CDC

Creative Hearts International (CHI)
Transforming Body, Mind and Business
to Match Spirit
209-814-4899
beverly@creativehearts.com
www.creativehearts.com

Beverly awakens souls to the truth of their unique brilliance. She has built and led worldwide teams toward their individual and organizational greatness. She has worked in the corporate and non-profit world since 1982 where she developed and utilized effective leadership and business planning processes.

Bev has a master's degree in administration and organizational management. She is a Certified Dream Coach®, One Page Business Plan® consultant, Simple Spiritual Energy practitioner, program facilitator, inspirational speaker and licensed True Purpose™ coach. She is also the author of *The Three Reasons*.

Bev is the founder and CEO of Creative Hearts International, which provides transformational life and business services and products for individuals and organizations looking for the clarity of purpose that will change the world. She is also the founder of women who wear their power™, a unique and transformational program that introduces women to their potential and untapped inner power. Bev leads a movement of powerful women transforming body, mind and business to match their Spirit, inviting them to join her as active and lifelong members of the Joyful Millionaire Circle. Visit www.creativehearts.com/catchyourstar for your *free* Women of Power Ritual Pak (a $97 value)!

Be a Leader—
Live Your Passion!

By Courtney Hawkins

Imagine living the life that you were destined to live, knowing that who you are matters because you have optimized your full potential. When you discover your natural born leadership skills and consciously embrace all that you are and are meant to be, your true journey of living your passion begins.

I have worked with hundreds of women to identify and capture the natural born leader inside of them as a means to living their passion. Through this process, I have harnessed my leadership skills and used them to catapult me to success as a top-level leader of a prominent direct sales company. Setting forth on this journey of living your passion begins by discovering your innate leader skill set which allows you to achieve personal and professional success like never before!

When you hear the word *leader,* what pops into your mind? Do you think of a specific person? Character traits? Do you ever wonder if leaders are born or made? Does everyone have what it takes to be a leader? Does everyone have a leadership skill set ready to be discovered? These are some of the ideas we'll explore in this chapter.

Maybe your entrepreneurial spirit manifested itself at a very young age. Like many others, I always had a desire to be more and do more when I was a child. Whether it was operating a lemonade stand, selling Girl Scout cookies, coordinating a neighborhood talent show, writing a neighborhood newspaper or setting up a nail polish stand on the side on the road, I always had a business in the making. Most of the neighborhood kids called me "bossy," however, I liked to think of it as leadership skills in the making.

I believe that we are each born with a unique set of strengths, gifts, attributes and talents. One of my strengths is the ability to stimulate and motivate others. I have the uncanny ability to raise the energy in a room and create momentum and movement. One of my dear friends calls it the Pied Piper effect. I am loud, energetic and positive. I thrive on enlivening, enlarging and encouraging other people's visions. I am also a connector. I am passionate about connecting and weaving people together so that they can get together and create something phenomenal. The most amazing part about making connections is that it is not at all about me. It is about the people being connected. It is about the people being affected. It is about the people being changed.

Once I realized my unique skill sets, it allowed me to live and work in my strength area. My goal is to inspire women to live their passion and empower them to financial freedom. I am able to use this positioning statement as a litmus test for everything I do.

"The two most important days in your life are the day you were born and the day you discover why you were born."
—**Mark Twain, American author and humorist**

Identifying your strengths and shining qualities is the first step toward discovering your natural born leadership and living your passion. Ask your closest friends and family to describe you.

Compare what they say and see if there are commonalities. Think about the moments when you have been at your very happiest. What were you doing at the time? Often, during the moments in your life when you feel your best, you are utilizing one of your strengths.

Strength areas could be an ability to inspire. Perhaps you have a visionary mindset or an understanding of how things and people work. Maybe you are good at analyzing facts and making projections.

Capture Your Natural Born Leadership

I have identified five steps to help you capture your natural born leadership.

1. Find Your Spoon. Once you have identified your personal list of strengths, it is important to attach them to your spoon. Your spoon? Why yes, your spoon—the very thing that stirs you. It is what sets you in to motion. Your spoon knows no limits or fear. Have you ever participated in or watched a game of Spoons? It is a fast-paced game involving cards and spoons. The object of the game is to have a spoon at the end of each round and ultimately be the player with the final spoon. The game of Spoons is competitive and fun. Those playing take risks and become unleashed.

It is the same with your spoon. It is the thing that stirs you at the core. It is that emotion at the center of your being that truly defines who you are and what makes you tick. Some people call this your "why." I would call it your "why not?"

Children's literature is full of amazing life lessons. One of my favorite children's books is called Spoon by Amy Krause Rosenthal. In this book, the main character, a spoon, compares himself to all the other utensils. He does not notice his own unique set of strengths and attributes because he is too busy wishing he was something else. We tend to do that same thing. We are so busy comparing ourselves to others and thinking about the qualities that we do not have, that we fail to see how our very own spoon qualities are exactly what we need to create something magnificent!

2. Celebrate! The second step toward capturing your Natural Born Leadership and living your passion is learning to celebrate! It might seem like such a simple concept, however it really is what sets apart the good from the great. It is what I believe separates a leader from the crowd.

Celebrating is a lifestyle. It is a cognitive choice to celebrate what is and not mourn what is not. It is choosing to focus on the positive at all times. It is living out loud—the concept that the glass is more than half full. The glass also contains the best tasting water in the world and the glass itself is the most beautiful glass ever created.

Do not get me wrong. Life is not perfect. Many obstacles and distractions will be thrown our way. It is your choice to celebrate or to mourn. My life has been far from perfect, yet I choose to celebrate!

When you choose to celebrate, you create a culture of gratitude and success. That culture can be created within your friendships, your family and your business relationships. When you consistently speak positive words and choose to celebrate and not mourn, you *exponentialize* the joy in your life and in the lives of others.

I believe people who celebrate implement two key factors into their daily lives. I like to call the first factor the *Stickwithitness Factor.* In other words, they do not give up! No matter what the challenge or obstacle, they face it knowing that whatever it is, it will not defeat them. They declare victory over every challenge and celebrate every step of the way. The wishy-washies disappear because those with the Stickwithitness Factor are confident and persistent and always stick with it!

I call the second factor the *Feng Shui Factor.* This factor allows you to rid your life of things and people who are not uplifting, encouraging or positive. Every now and then, it is important to take an inventory of those with whom you spend your time. Ask yourself if they are moving you toward your dreams and allowing you to be the best you that you can be. (see Jane Inch's chapter, Finding Your Voice on page 43)

"You are the average of the five people you spend the most time with."
—Jim Rohn, American entrepreneur, author
and motivational speaker

Take a snapshot of your week and identify who is influencing your thinking patterns. Sometimes, those with whom we spend the most time are not filling our emotional buckets or encouraging and inspiring us to be the best that we can be. What do you do? I do not recommend that you go and get an entirely new set of friends. However, I do think it is important that you surround yourself with people who adopt your celebration philosophy. Begin by seeking out family members, friends and business acquaintances who will hold you accountable to your celebration philosophy and are committed to your success both personally and professionally.

A friend of mine once shared an idea with me that we should each have our own personal board of directors. The concept was genius to me! I was so excited to develop my own personal board to whom I could go for advice, clarity, perspective and truth. I created my own personal board of men and women whom I respect immensely. I know that they have my best interest in mind and close to their heart. I selected people to fill specific roles on my board—each utilizing their personal strengths.

My husband is the chairman of my board. He loves me unconditionally and knows my greatest assets and my biggest flaws. One of his strengths is the ability to see through the drama and the muck of life and accurately see actions and people for what and who they are.

He has the amazing ability to look past what things may seem to be and pinpoint what things really are. He is able to steer me and my decisions in healthy and functional directions. Having him on my board is essential to keeping me centered and grounded as a wife, mother, friend and businesswoman.

My board of directors knows me. They know my wildest dreams and my deepest fears. They celebrate with me and keep me on the path of positivity! I encourage you to develop your own personal board of directors. These people could be your family, friends, co-workers or business mentors. This process may take some time. Be patient and diligent, knowing that your personal board will be instrumental in your future.

3. Be authentic. The third step toward capturing your Natural Born Leadership and living your passion is to be authentic. There is only one you and only you can do what you can do! Authenticity requires knowing who you are and being who you are with consistency and integrity. When you show up, wherever you are, decide to show up as the real you. You only have one chance to make a first impression. The rest of the time, you are building credibility and trust.

The single best way to be authentic is to live according to your heart values. Your heart values are the things in life most precious to you. What is most important to you? What kind of legacy do you want to leave? Think about these questions and answer them honestly.

For me, this was a very emotional discovery. My faith and my family have always been my heart values. However, my day-to-day life did not authentically reflect these heart values. By definition, being a true leader means that people are following. Everyone wants to follow someone who is trustworthy, credible and living in accordance to their own heart values.

When I was in second grade, we learned the "Be Verbs." We used to chant rhythmically "am, is, are, was, were, be, being, been!" One of the best ways to be an authentic leader is to live as a be verb. Whatever it is that needs to be done or is being done or has been done, you must have been there, done it and are willing to do it again! People must be able to relate to you and to trust you. When you are authentic, you become transparent. Transparency invites others to see you for who you really are without any walls or facades. Others will not only trust you, they will follow you because of your authenticity in every situation. The consistency that your authenticity brings to relationships are refreshing and comforting to you and those you lead.

4. Connect with others. Learning to connect is the fourth step toward living your passion by discovering your natural born leader. Connecting with other people requires utilizing effective communication skills such as active listening, empathy and asking probing questions. Connecting also draws on your ability to look beyond yourself and personal interests and truly desire to develop others. True connecting takes practice and consistent effort.

As a speech language pathologist, one of the activities I had to do during one of my graduate school clinicals was to measure the amount of time I spent talking versus the amount of time my clients talked during a therapy session. I was surprised to learn that I talked almost four times the amount of my speech therapy client! I learned that I needed to spend more time listening and less time talking. It was a lesson I never forgot and carried over into my leadership role. In a true effort to connect, I had to learn to spend more time actively listening, empathizing and asking questions.

My husband shared another valuable and priceless life lesson with me which has strengthened my ability to connect with others. "Sometimes," he shared, "things aren't out there. They are right there—in front of you. Be present and do not miss opportunities, because they only happen once. If you don't take advantage of the moment, it will be gone."

Those words resonated with me and I make choices to connect and engage with people and seize every opportunity as it is presented, knowing that this might be the only opportunity to connect. I know that when I am choosing to engage in one activity, I am choosing to not spend my time and energy doing something else. Focusing your attention and truly connecting with those you are with will solidify the meaningful relationships in your life and allow you to impact others in a powerful way.

5. Embrace your inner awesomeness! The final step toward acquiring your natural born leadership and then living your passion is to embrace your inner awesomeness! Your natural leader is within you. She is alive. She is waiting. She is fabulous. Find her and you will discover all that you are and who you can be.

It is time to begin your journey of leading and living your true passion. I encourage you to travel through the five steps outlined in this chapter. Find your spoon and develop a lifestyle of celebration. Be your authentic self and connect with others. Finally, embrace your inner awesomeness and you can capture the natural born leader within you!

Courtney Hawkins

727-642-3619
courtney@achievesuccesswithcourtney.com
www.achievesuccesswithcourtney.com

Achiever, believer and natural born leader, Courtney Hawkins lives her life positively impacting others. Her early entrepreneurial spirit manifested itself into a thriving business opportunity that has allowed her to share this gift with thousands of other women. Her most meaningful and impactful contributions have been her privilege to inspire women to live their passion and empower them to financial freedom.

Courtney holds a bachelor's of science in biology and a master's of science in communication disorders and sciences. She is a licensed speech language pathologist and holds her Certificate of Clinical Competency through the American Speech and Hearing Association.

Courtney's successes include being a founding consultant of Thirty-One® Gifts and one of the first twenty women to achieve the highest ranking title as a Senior Executive Director. In 2007, she was appointed a member of the Presidential Advisory Council and has served on the Leadership Council for four years as a Top Bonus Earner and Top Dreambuilder. One of her proudest achievements was being featured as a Circle of Honor Member.

Courtney speaks at leadership summits and professional and personal development opportunities. Presently, she leads a multi-million dollar downline team of over 14,000 women.

Stop Hiding and Shine!

By Rebecca Hall Gruyter

I believe each of us has been given our own unique talents, abilities, gifts and dreams that need to be shared with the world.

Have you ever had a dream? Something that was placed in your heart? Something big that you felt or feel called to do? I did. My dream started to develop within me in high school. In this chapter, I'll share with you where this dream came from and how I stepped into it. Then I'll share some steps to show how you can stop hiding and shine!

> *"Everyone has talent. What is rare is the courage*
> *to follow that talent wherever it leads."*
> **—Erica Jong, American author and teacher**

From the ages of six through twelve, I lived in an abusive and neglectful environment. It was unsafe to be seen or heard, therefore I learned to hide behind smiles and act like everything was okay when in fact, it was not. As the years wore on, I began to believe I did not matter and that it was my fault. I was not loveable nor worth protecting. I was unsafe and lived in constant sadness and fear. Survival meant not being seen or heard.

Finally, the truth came out and I was rescued by my birthfather and moved in with him and my wonderful stepmother, who became the mother of my heart. I started to walk through healing. Now I was in a safe place and was given the opportunity to be loved and protected by a family who wanted and loved me. I learned that I mattered, it was not my fault, and that those things I had begun to believe were lies, not truth. I began to find my voice. (see Jane Inch's chapter, Finding Your Voice on page 43)

As I found my voice, I learned that other little girls and women had similar experiences to mine, however they continued to believe the lies. This started the fire in the belly for me. I wanted to rescue them from the lies, for them to know the truth that they are beautifully and wonderfully made—that they do matter, they are loveable, that they should be seen and heard!

> *"No one can make you feel inferior without your consent."*
> **—Eleanor Roosevelt, former First Lady of the Unites States,**
> **writer, humanitarian**

I had the opportunity to attend a Christian women's conference in Sacramento where I saw powerful women take the stage and share their stories and messages. I felt how it affected me—I laughed and cried. I was encouraged and moved. My life was richer and I had more courage on my path because of all that they had shared with us. My dream was born. I rushed home from the event and shared with my mom, "Mom, Mom! I know what I want to do with my life— the way I can help people and make a difference! I want to be a motivational speaker!" I felt called to encourage women, to lift them up with truth, to set them free from lies. To have my journey help others in a powerful way. To show them the truth and that they can heal, be powerful and walk in joy and love.

Have you ever had a dream move you in powerful ways that leaves you knowing this is it? How often have you felt excited about a dream only to have "reality" set in? That happened to me. My mom gently shared with me that I had to stand in front of people and speak if I were to share a message with them and motivate them. I was crushed! I let the dream fade a bit. Has that happened to you?

Here's what happened to me. I had found my voice and could share from my heart at home and sometimes one on one. However, I was not able to share in front of groups. I believe as my mind, heart and soul healed, my body still remembered the bad times and was trying to protect me. Therefore, when I tried to speak in class, stand up and say my name, or answer a question, I could barely squeak out my name. I would turn bright red. My hands and knees would shake and I would get sweaty. My eyes would water and blur and my voice would become lost.

> *"What is very difficult at first, if we keep on trying, gradually becomes easier."*
> **—Helen Keller, American author, political activist and lecturer**

This frustrated me and I pushed myself. As I went through college and moved into the work force, I pushed myself to interact with people. I put myself into leadership opportunities and took speaking courses. One of the greatest gifts a speaking instructor shared with me was that the audience actually wants you to share your message. They want to hear your voice and are supporting you. They want to see you having fun on stage. It was a totally new perspective for me and gave me a lot of courage. It helped me begin to come out from hiding.

As I climbed the ladder and built a successful career, I also found that I was frustrated that I did not feel I was making a difference about things that really mattered for me. Sure, I was sharing valuable information, however I was not connecting and moving them at a heart level. You see, I had let my dream become logical and something I could control or create. I had settled for just making a positive difference and communicating to large groups. I had forgotten my dream and let it become smaller, manageable and safe.

I sought training and coaches to help me become more skilled and comfortable speaking with microphones or on stages, in front of groups of all sizes, on interviews and radio. Still, I discovered I was continuing to hide—still trying to stay safe and not be seen. I had learned the skill of hiding in the public eye.

> *"Don't compromise yourself. You're all you've got."*
> **—Janis Joplin, American singer and songwriter**

Finally, two of my mentors truly saw me. I shared my list of goals: I wanted to connect with people in a deeper and more effective way. I wanted to touch them in their heart and help them move toward action. I did not just want to share information; I wanted to make a difference. They kindly put their arm around me and told me they could help me make the heart connection with my audience. However, they explained that I had to be willing to stop hiding. They told me I cannot make a medium-control difference. They held a much bigger vision for me and believed I was called to stand and share in a bigger way.

My mentors helped me discover that those roles, suits, jewelry, image and information I was hiding behind to protect and shield me were actually keeping people from me. Those things were preventing people from seeing or hearing me—my true self, my true voice. They said that they would hold the bigger vision for me until I could see it for myself. They asked if I was "in." I said "Yes!" I had to be willing to be vulnerable and authentic if I was going to connect and make a difference on a heart level. I was terrified, yet I did say yes and was in with knees knocking and voice shaking.

At first, my mentors stood in front of me showing me it was safe. Then they stood beside me, cheering me on. Then finally, they stood behind me and pushed me out of the nest into my light. I am so grateful for them and their not letting me settle for a medium and controlled impact. In addition to my financial practice, I became a coach and workshop leader, a speaker and a wife. I was connecting with people on a deeper level—finally making more of a difference.

> *"If your experiences would benefit anybody,*
> *give them to someone."*
> **—Florence Nightingale, American pioneer of modern nursing**

Over the next several months and years, I faced some life-changing events. My husband had a motorcycle accident and I was in a car accident. Both resulted in injuries. These events challenged me to let go of actions and beliefs that I was holding onto so tightly and to step out more into trusting the process of *stop hiding and step into light.*

I was recently asked to speak on stage at an event. There were going to be more than 150 people in the audience. As I prepared for the presentation in which I would share my story, my journey and encourage others to step into their dreams, my mom called and asked what was going on.

So many things raced through my mind as I was thinking about what I should share with her. Should I share with her that my Women's Empowerment Series has grown so big that not only are we looking for a new space that can fit all of those attending, that we're actually expanding to the Sacramento area? Should I share with her that I am a co-author of two books to be released this year on a local and national level? Should I share with her that I have two radio interviews coming up? Should I share with her that I would be speaking at an upcoming event where I would be sharing my story with 150 or more attendees? Should I share with her that later this summer I would be standing on stage in front of thousands of women being recognized as a speaker and best selling author? All this from her little girl who could barely stand up in class and share her name in high school?

Instead, I decided to ask her if she remembered my dream in high school of becoming a motivational speaker. She became kind of quiet and careful in her response, as that had been a really difficult time for all of us. She replied, "Yes, Rebecca, I remember." I replied, "Mom, I want to share with you that it's happening now." We laughed, cried, and celebrated!

> *"Never lose your zeal for building a better world."*
> **—May McLeod Bethune, American educator**
> **and Civil Rights leader**

The next day, I stood on stage and shared that my name was Rebecca Hall Gruyter, founder and owner of Your Purpose Driven Practice. I have the honor and privilege of empowering women and in doing so transforming lives. I shared my story and even the conversation I had the day before with my mom. I ended the presentation with the same message I want to share with you...

You may have forgotten your dream, your calling. Perhaps you let your dream become smaller, more palatable, more "grown-up and real." I want you to know that your dream or calling can become a reality for you. My dream to become a motivational speaker seemed impossible when I could barely stand up and say my name. Yet, it has come true.

I want to stand in front of you and show you it's safe to dream again and honor your calling. Then, I want to stand beside you and cheer you on, and then, I will stand behind you and push you out of the nest into your light.

> *"Your passion is waiting for your courage to catch up."*
> **—Marilyn Greist, American corporate trainer**

Five Steps to Step into Your Light

Following are some strategies I have learned along the way.

1. Stop and get still. Ask yourself, "What am I feeling pull at my heart? What is it that I feel called to do?"

2. Define success. What does success look like for you? What does it feel like? What does it do for you? How does it tap into your dream or calling on your heart?

2. Uncover your gifts or talents. What are some things people say you are good at doing? What are some of your weaknesses?

3. Play to your strengths. How can you start "playing" more to your strengths? What are things you like doing and are good at doing? How can you invest your time in things that bring you more energy and do more of the things you are uniquely gifted to do? Are you building a life and your work in a way that is built around who you are, around how you are uniquely made?

4. Get support. Find a coach, friend or mentor who can see and hold a bigger vision for you. Find someone who will support you in moving toward your dream or vision—toward that which you are called to do. What is one thing you can do today that will help you move closer toward playing to your strengths and talents?

5. Take action. Take the step, even with knees knocking. Then find the next step you can take and repeat.

People are waiting to hear your message, see you, and receive your unique gifts and talents. No one else can take your place and share your message in the way they need to hear it. When you then stand in front of your people, you can show them it is safe. Then, you stand beside them cheering them on and then, you get to stand behind them and push them out of the nest and into their light.

This is how we create a ripple effect transforming our lives and those we are called to touch. I want to inspire and encourage you to answer the call. Step toward and into your dream—with knees knocking. *Stop hiding and step into your light!*

Rebecca Hall Gruyter
Your Purpose Driven Practice
Empowering Women, Transforming Lives.

925-787-1572
rebecca@yourpurposedrivenpractice.com
www.yourpurposedrivenpractice.com

Rebecca Hall Gruyter is the founder of Your Purpose Driven Practice, a Character Code™ Coach Master Trainer, creator of Your Success Formula™, and owner of two successful private practices. She is passionate about helping women accelerate their business resulting in more of the right clients, higher income and more profits. She has been giving presentations, seminars and workshops since 1995, and specializes in aligning your business with you, your core values, and your passions so that you can impact the world in a big way.

As a speaker, empowerment leader, teacher, business owner and coach, Rebecca is committed to her clients having their message and voice be heard. She is known for her authenticity and her ability to synthesize complex information into an easy-to-follow plan that everyone enjoys.

Rebecca wants to lift up women leaders—those with a call on their heart to empower others. If you would like to learn more about Rebecca or would like to share with her the call on your heart; please go to www.yourpurposedrivenpractice.com and schedule a free half-hour discovery session. Remember to step into your brilliance and let your light shine!

More *Catch Your Star*

Now that you have learned about many ways to catch your star, the next step is to take action. Get started applying what you have learned in the pages of this book.

We want you to know that we are here to help and inspire you to meet your personal objectives. The following pages list our geographical locations. Regardless of where we are located, many of us provide a variety of services over the phone or through webinars, and we welcome the opportunity to travel to your location or invite you to ours.

You can find out more about each of us by reading our bios at the end of our chapters, or by visiting our websites listed there and on the following pages.

When you are ready for one-on-one consulting or group training from any of the co-authors in this book, we are available! When you call us, let us know you have read our book, and we will provide you with a free phone consultation to determine your needs and how to best serve you.

Geographical Listings for *Catch Your Star*

Canada

Alberta
Tammy Rose Phye www.lifestyleharmony.ca

Ontario
Lauren Carbis lauren@lifescapeimage.com

United States

California
Beverly Adamo www.creativehearts.com
Tobey Allen www.seedsofpossibilitiescoaching.com
Jean Kathryn Carlson www.wakeuptovibrantliving.com
Angeli Raven Fitch www.fitchcriminaldefense.com
Rebecca Hall Gruyter www.yourpurposedrivenpractice.com
Sonia Hassey www.inspiredfuturescoach.com
Paula-Jo Husack www.leadlifenow.com
Jane Inch www.janeinch.com
Maggie Schreiber www.wow-womenofwonder.com
Erin Summ www.erinsumm.com

Connecticut
Jadwiga Pylak   www.meditationandpeace.com

Florida
Courtney Hawkins   www.achievesuccesswithcourtney.com

New Jersey
Laurie Leinwand   www.ideas2action-coaching.com

Texas
Linda Ballesteros   www.lindaballesteros.com
Michelle Barr   www.theartoftakingaction.com
Nora Cabrera   www.noracabrera.com
Shontaye Hawkins   www.emergencesuccess.com
Anne Kjellgren   www.yourrapidturnaround.com
Dr. Yvette Nadeau   www.totalchirocare.com

About THRIVE Publishing™

THRIVE Publishing develops books for experts who want to share their knowledge with more and more people. We provide our co-authors with a proven system, professional guidance and support, producing quality, multi-author, how-to books that uplift and enhance the personal and professional lives of the people they serve.

We know that getting a book written and published is a huge undertaking. To make that process as easy as possible, we have an experienced team with the resources and know-how to put a quality, informative book in the hands of our co-authors quickly and affordably. Our co-authors are proud to be included in THRIVE Publishing™ books because these publications enhance their business missions, give them a professional outreach tool and enable them to communicate essential information to a wider audience.

You can find out more about our upcoming book projects at
www.thrivebooks.com

Other Books from
THRIVE Publishing™

For more information on
Power to Change and *Incredible Life*, visit:
www.thrivebooks.com/store

You're Invited...

Catch Your Star

Top Experts Share Insights for Lifelong Fulfillment

Bev Adamo • Tobey Allen • Linda Ballesteros • Michelle Barr • Nora Cabrera
Lauren Carbis • Jean Kathryn Carlson • Angeli Fitch • Rebecca Hall Gruyter
Sonia Hassey • Courtney Hawkins • Shontaye Hawkins • Paula-Jo Husack
Jane Inch • Anne Kjellgren • Laurie Leinwand • Dr. Yvette Nadeau • Tammy Phye
Jadwiga Pylak • Maggie Schreiber • Erin Summ

For more copies of this book, *Catch Your Star:
Top Experts Share Insights for Lifelong Fulfillment*
contact any of the co-authors or visit
www.thrivebooks.com/store